My Case for Heaven

RICHARD M. BONGIOVANNI

iUniverse, Inc.
Bloomington

My Case for Heaven

iUniverse books may be ordered through booksellers or by contacting:

iUniverse
1663 Liberty Drive
Bloomington, IN 47403
www.iuniverse.com
1-800-Authors (1-800-288-4677)

*Because of the dynamic nature of the Internet, any web addresses or
links contained in this book may have changed since publication and
may no longer be valid. The views expressed in this work are solely those
of the author and do not necessarily reflect the views of the publisher,
and the publisher hereby disclaims any responsibility for them.*

*Any people depicted in stock imagery provided by Thinkstock are models,
and such images are being used for illustrative purposes only.*

Certain stock imagery © Thinkstock.

ISBN: 978-1-4620-2767-5 (sc)
ISBN: 978-1-4620-2769-9 (hc)
ISBN: 978-1-4620-2768-2 (e)

Printed in the United States of America

iUniverse rev. date: 08/16/2011

To my granddaughter Lisa for preparation of the illustrations and typing of the manuscript, and to my son Robert for helping me better organize the content.

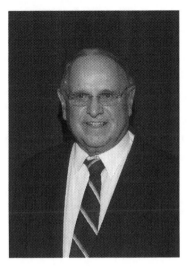

About the Author

The author, his family, and friends have personally experienced psychic phenomena, including ghosts, psychic readings, and past-life hypnosis. He has performed extensive research on the Bible miracles, miracles of the saints, modern miracles, psychic phenomena, ghosts, and prophets of the past and present. His background as a scientist has enabled him to combine these results to provide definite proof that heaven does indeed exist.

The author has received excellent reviews on his previous book, *Mentors to the Romans: The Search for the Etruscans* (see the back cover).

Contents

Acknowledgments

I would like to acknowledge the help given to me by my family, friends, and psychics for their input on their paranormal experiences, which I used in the personal experiences parts of the book. All illustrations are by the author.

Introduction

Do heaven and paranormal phenomena exist? In this book, I present strong evidence of their actual existence. I set out on my own personal journey to answer these difficult questions, and I found many things that surprised me. In the end, I discovered the most surprising thing of all: I am a believer.

A good friend of mine, who knew he was dying, kept asking me the same questions over and over again. "Why are we here? Where are we going when we die? What's it like there?" He wouldn't accept the standard answers, so I decided to research the subject. I have always been interested in the paranormal. At the age of sixteen, I decided to have a psychic friend of the family do a reading for me, which has, to date, turned out the way she predicted. I had read several books on psychic phenomena and have had several precognitive dreams, which have also been proven accurate.

For some people, faith is enough. They need no further proof because they have the certainty of their convictions. But for others, like my friend and I, there is a longing for further proof that the stories told in the Bible and other stories on faith are verifiable by other means and that there is some level of objective evidence.

I decided to base this book on the miracles of the Bible and the saints, modern miracles, angels and demons, psychic phenomena, ghosts and near-death experiences of heaven. Over the years, I have had a fascination with these topics, and they have deepened my own questioning and my own process of discovery. In each instance, I supply written or archeological proof of the miracles that I have found most convincing.

Although I cannot claim to have irrefutable evidence backing every belief, the evidence I did find was compelling. First, I studied the Bible. Genesis is remarkably accurate with the order that different life-forms appeared on Earth. The Bible, from Noah to the fall of Israel, has substantiation through historical and archeological finds in Egypt, the eastern Mediterranean, and Iraq. The places where Jesus performed his sermons and miracles still remain. Are there dependable, objective witnesses to Jesus's appearance? An ancient document describes him. Hundreds of well-documented miracles and healings performed by the saints are discussed. The modern miracles of Fatima and Lourdes offer further proof of divine intervention that have brought me to a place of belief.

Documented cases of angelic appearances are given, and exorcism of Satan and his demons offers proof of heaven and hell. Prophecies of the Bible, past prophets, and modern prophets are reviewed. Strangely enough, several of them made the same predictions of major catastrophes although they lived at different times—for example, the start of both World Wars, the atomic bomb, the first satellite, space travel, and the Kennedy assassination. Many dire predictions of the future are also discussed.

Finally, reincarnation, astral travel, and ghosts are examined; and a description of heaven is given based on Revelation and near-death experiences.

For some people—the hardened skeptics—no level of evidence will ever be accepted as proof. But for the open-minded, proof is available. For me, this material has transformed me from a pure scientist to a pilgrim in life.

CHAPTER 1

Creation

Genesis

Our little planet earth is just a speck, a mere 8,000 miles in diameter, compared to the size of the sun and some of the larger planets in our Milky Way Galaxy. Our sun is nearly a million miles in diameter; Jupiter, 88,000 miles; and Neptune, 27,700 miles. We are on a small spaceship traveling around the sun at sixty-four thousand miles per hour. Our solar system is traveling around the center of our Milky Way Galaxy at forty-five thousand miles per hour. Even at that speed, it takes us 200 million years to make the orbit around our galaxy's center. The Milky Way would appear like a giant Fourth of July pinwheel in slow motion if we could view it from the top. On a clear night, we see it as a thick band of stars extending up into the sky, because our solar system is near the rim and tilted at an angle of sixty-two degrees from the galactic plane.

Scientists estimate that the universe was created 14.5 billion years ago, when something smaller than an atom exploded. This is extremely hard for me to understand since it goes well beyond the laws of physics. How could anything so small have created something as huge as the universe? One may ask, "What is the universe?" Scientists estimate that our Milky Way Galaxy could contain more than 100 billion stars and that there are more than 100 billion galaxies in the universe. If you multiple the two figures together, you come up with a figure with twenty-two zeros for the possible number of stars in the universe. Many of these stars have exploded, and we see their remains as glowing balls of debris or rings, like those formed from cigarettes smoke. Some emit pulses of light many times a second, like a lighthouse, after they collapse.

Some are hundreds of times bigger than our sun. Scientists predict that our sun will explode in a few billion years, scorching all the planets in our solar system. Our sun is a huge thermonuclear reactor burning millions of tons of hydrogen gas every second. Yet it is so massive that it will take billions of years to burn up all of its hydrogen.

Stars are formed when the debris of other exploding stars collapses due to the force of gravity. They start out as bright young blue stars; some become yellow dwarfs like our sun. Others become red dwarfs, which are slowly burning up their hydrogen fuel and may survive for tens of billions of years. Some, such as white dwarfs, have expended all their hydrogen fuel and are becoming cold. Our sun will become a red giant star one hundred times larger than it presently is—so large that it will extend past the orbits of earth and Mars, vaporizing everything in its path. After ejecting all of its outer layers, it will become a small white dwarf. Rarely, stars will become super giants, some as large as 600 million miles in diameter, six hundred times the size of our sun.

Our closest star, Proxima Centuri, is 4.3 light-years away, nearly 26 trillion miles. Between our solar system and the nearest star, there is a vast emptiness of nothingness. The closest large galaxy, Andromeda, is two million light-years away. Needless to say, unless we invent a prolusion system that allows us to travel at the speed of light, we will never visit the stars or other extraterrestrial planets. Scientists are now testing a prototype ion engine that could possibly reach such a speed.[1]

Since the 1960s, astronomers have had no success in the search for alien life outside of our solar system. The Society for Extraterrestrial Investigation (SETI) astronomers have been listening for a return from radio signals they have been directing to stars, which they have suspected of having alien life. This has been the only available method since the earthbound telescopes are obscured by our atmosphere, and the Hubble Space Telescope was not designed to search for planets.

The recently launched Kepler planet-finder telescope has been designed to make direct images of earth-like planets around the closest stars. Scientists are using two methods to detect planets. One is by direct imaging—a planet blocks its star's light as is passes in front of its star. The second is by observing if the planet pulls its star from side to side far enough to be observed. This can only be applied to large planets that are massive enough to affect the stars orbit.[2]

Once a new planet has been detected, astronomers use several criteria to determine if it can support life. First, its star has to be at least 3 billion years old (determined by color and size). Stars that are less than 3 billion years old are too young to have planets, which could evolve life, since our sun is 4.2 billion years old.

1   Levy, Skywatching.
2   National Geographic, December 2009.

Second, stars that are more than 1.5 times the mass of our sun would burn out before life can develop. Third, the planet has to be the ideal distance from the star. Too close and it will be too hot to support life, like the planet Mercury; too far, it will be too cold to support life, like the planet Mars. Once a likely planet is discovered, scientists can use instruments to determine if it has the correct amounts of oxygen, carbon dioxide, and water to support plant and animal life.[3]

According to scientists working on the Kepler telescope, over 1,200 stars with planets orbiting around them have been discovered to date but none that would be habitable. These planets are merely huge balls of gas, similar to Jupiter and Saturn, or coated with ice hundreds of miles thick or dry and barren, similar to the moon. None are suitable for life like our little planet is. It took the exact combination of water, temperature, soil, and air to produce life. When I think about the improbability of this being pure chance, I feel, at a deep level, that this had to be created by a great intelligence—God. The Bible does not give any dates for creation of life on Earth. It does give a date for the creation of Adam and Eve as being 4000 BC, but I believe that this was because Jewish genealogy only went back that far. Strangely enough, the order of the days in Genesis agrees remarkably with geological periods of earth discovered by scientists. *"One thousand years being but a day to God."*

---

3   Wikipedia

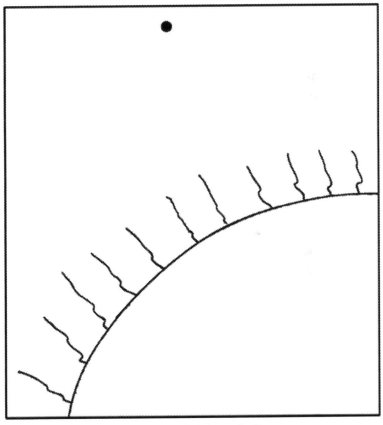

Size of the Earth Relative to the Sun

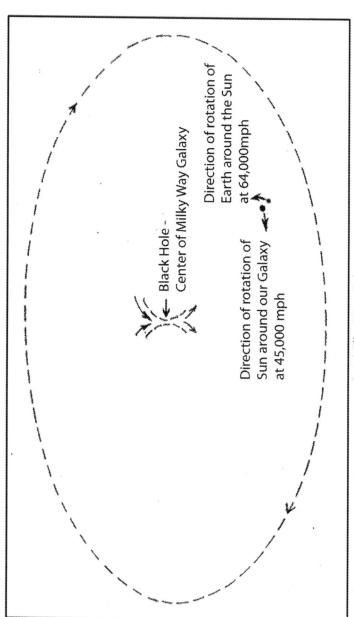

Black Hole - Center of Milky Way Galaxy

Direction of rotation of Earth around the Sun at 64,000mph

Direction of rotation of Sun around our Galaxy at 45,000 mph

Our Milky Way Galaxy

It seems very unlikely that earth-bound people five thousand years ago could have coincidentally described an order of creation that so closely mirrors the findings of modern science.

Genesis 1:2–5	The first day, God created the earth and the sea, and then God said, "Let there be light." The sun, moon, and stars had been created; but they were not yet visible, because the earth's crust was so hot that the oceans were boiling, creating a fog so that they could not be seen. This agrees with the Precambrian era 4.5 to 5 billion years ago, when the earth was formed.
Genesis 1:6–8	The second day, God created dry land and the atmosphere. In the Cambrian and Silurian, 600 to 400 million years ago, dry land appeared.
Genesis 1:9–13	The third day, God created the grass, herbs, and trees, which developed into immense tropical jungles. Many submersions in sediment caused by rising and falling seas caused the plants to turn to coal and oil. This agrees with the Devonian period 400 million to 250 million years ago.
Genesis 1:14–19	The fourth day, God made the sun, stars, and moon appear. He had already created the sun, moon, and stars 5–6 billion years ago, when he created the universe; but they now appeared for the first time as the fog lifted. This would relate to the Pennsylvanian period 250 million years ago.
Genesis 1:20–25	The fifth day, God created the fishes, sea animals (amphibians), and birds. This agrees with the Mesozoic period, 230–65 million years ago.

Genesis 1:24–31	The sixth day, God created the land animals and man. During the Cenozoic, Miocene, Pleistocene, and Holocene periods, 50 million years ago to date, the land animals and man appeared.
Genesis 2:1–3	The seventh day, God rested and proclaimed that this day should be a day of worship.
Genesis 2:8	*Then the Lord God planted a garden eastward in Eden; and there he put the man whom he had formed.*
Genesis 2:9	*And out of the ground made the Lord God to grow every tree that is pleasant to the sight, and good for food.*
Genesis 2:10	*And a river went out of Eden to water the garden; and from hence it was parted and went into four heads.*
Genesis 2:11	*The name of the first river is Pison [Araxes]… the land where there is gold.*
Genesis 2:13	*The name of the second river is Gihon [Kura]*
Genesis 2:14	*The Name of the third river is Hiddekel [Tigris], and the name of the fourth river is Euphrates*
Genesis 2:19	*And out of the ground the Lord God formed every beast of the field, and every fowl of the air.*

Although it is not objective evidence, it is interesting to note that other traditions have noted creation stories quite like the story told in Genesis. The Bible describes, in detail, the story of creation, but are there any other references to the story? Clay tablets have been found in many of the ancient cities of Iraq (Babylon) before the time of Abraham, which are strikingly similar to those stories of the Bible (i.e., "In the beginning the Gods made the upper and lower firmaments—the heavens and the earth. On the fourth day the stars appeared ... made the grass ... the beast of the fields and the cattle, and all living things. On the sixth day formed man out of the dust of the ground ... put man and wife in a garden ... they were unclothed ... the seventh day was appointed a holy day.") If more than one culture tells a similar story, it lends credence to the story being objectively true.

The Garden of Eden

Is there a known place on Earth—modern or ancient—that could match the biblical descriptions of Eden? This is a question that has long fascinated me. The Bible states it is the place where the Euphrates and three other rivers are united. The place where the Euphrates, the Tigris, the Araxes, and the Kura are united is in the Caucasus Mountains region of Armenia. It is the region where the ox, goat, pear, plum, cherry, berries, grapes, olives, figs, spinach, radish, onions, and most of the other fruits and vegetables come from. Armenia contains a variety of minerals, including silver and gold.

The Kingdom of Armenia has some of the most beautiful countryside in the world. Situated on a high plateau, it is surrounded by mountains and is well watered by rivers. Strangely enough, Mount Ararat, of Bible fame, rises to the east of the plateau. Fertile mountain pastures yield abundant crops of wheat, barley, millet, rye, sesame, flax, and grapevines. The highlands furnish excellent pasture for sheep, goats, and cattle. The region is also famous for its fine horses. Surely, Armenia could easily have been the "The Garden of Eden."[4]

---

4   Chahin, The Kingdom of Armenia.

The Bible (Genesis 21–31) states that the descendants of Shem, which includes the Jews, originally occupied the north Euphrates Valley and the area adjacent. This would include the land of Armenia, where the ark landed.

The Babylonians, who predated the ancient Hebrews, corroborate the Garden of Eden story in some respects. Babylonian inscriptions found on ancient clay tablets in Iraq refer to a tree of life, from which man was caused to depart, due to the influence of an evil serpent (Garden of Eden?). He was forbidden to return by guardian cherubs (angels with flaming swords). Another Babylonian inscription reads, "Near Eridu was a garden in which there was a mysterious sacred tree, a tree of life planted by the Gods ... protected by a guardian spirit, and no man enters."[5]

The Reason for Creation

In the beginning, God created Adam in his image and likeness so that he would have someone to love and who would return his love. For this same reason, he created Eve so that man would have someone to love and who would return his love.

People often ask, "What is the purpose of life?" Everything that happens to an individual is for a purpose. The main purposes of life are:

1. To love and to serve others. This would include our relatives, friends, neighbors, and the needy.

2. To gain knowledge. Some of us go on to become professionals, gaining our knowledge from books. Others' purpose in life is to raise a family and love and nurture our children.

---

5   Halley, Halley's Bible Handbook.

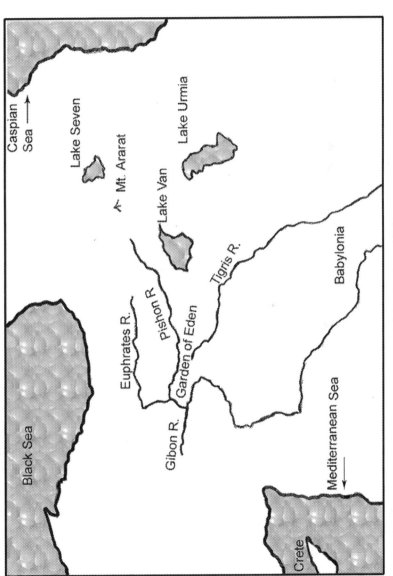

Location of the Garden of Eden

3. To grow spiritually. You don't need a religion to accomplish this. Believe that God is our creator and enjoy the beauty of nature that he has created for us.

4. Fulfill our life's mission. We all know that we have inherited certain talents by some mysterious means. Our mission is to develop these talents for our own good and for the good of others.

God gave us gifts above the animals:

1. A soul which would live forever with him

2. Intellect so that we could understand his works and serve him with our talents

3. Moral conscience to distinguish good from evil

4. Freedom of choice

5. An artistic sense that lets us appreciate beauty

6. A heart with which to experience love and all of our other emotions[6]

What is the difference between the spirit and the body's soul? In his book, Deepak Chopra believes that:

1. The body is the resting place of the spirit (Gen. 2:7).

2. The spirit thus becomes the soul of man (Gen. 2:7).

3. The spirit survives the death of the body and ascends into heaven or receives judgment on the final day (Eccles. 12:7).

---

6   Pache, The Future Life.

4. The spirit decides when, where, and who it will be reincarnated as, who its parents will be, and who it will marry. God decides how many children we will have and our time of death.[7]

Visions of God

If God appeared to a human being and was witnessed with human eyes, what would he look like? Would his appearance be like anything familiar to us now? These are questions I have asked myself, and I have looked in the Bible for answers. The prophets Daniel, Ezekiel, and Isaiah had visions of God sitting on his throne. Daniel describes him as "the ancient one," and Ezekiel describes him as having "the likeness of a man, enswathed in the glow of an incandescent light." Daniel describes his throne as being of "fiery flames and the wheels there of burning fire." Ezekiel describes the throne as being of blue sapphire and four immense whirling wheels of beryl, green precious stone: their rims full of eyes. Daniel states that "a fiery stream issued and came forth from before him." Ezekiel goes on to say that this device "moved like flashes of lighting from place to place with noise like the roar of the ocean."

To me, having a sense of what Jesus physically looked like makes his story seem more real. In Revelation, John had a vision of Jesus. He described him as one like the son of man, his hair white with the whiteness of wool, his eyes like a burning flame, his feet like burnished (polished) bronze, and his voice like the sound of the ocean, "His face was like the sun shining with all its force." Both Ezekiel and John describe God as shining with brilliant light (Ezek. 1:4, 2:8; Rev. 1:13–18, 4:2, 3; Dan. 7:9, 13).

---

7   Chopra, Life after Death.

It is interesting to note that all three of the prophets describe God as having the likeness of a man, which agrees with the statement that "God created man in his own likeness." In Genesis 1:26, 27, both Ezekiel and John, described a noise like "the roar of the ocean." The angels are also described as having "a voice like the roar of a crowd and shinning with intense light."

The prophets and other biblical authors had a vested interest in saying that Jesus actually lived. Are there other more objective sources that can supply a witness to Jesus's earthly life? It was a powerful moment for me when I came across just such a description of Jesus in a letter supposedly written by Publius Lentulus, a superior of Pontius Pilate, to the Roman Senate at the time of Jesus in *Halley's Bible Handbook*.[8]

In this time appeared a man endowed with great powers. His name is Jesus. His disciples call him the son of God. He is of noble and well-proportioned stature, with a face full of kindness, and yet firmness, so that beholders both love him and fear him. His hair is the color of wine, straight and without luster, but from the level of the ears curling and glossy. His forehead is even and smooth, his face without blemish, and enhanced by a tempered bloom, his countenance ingenious and kind. Nose and mouth are in no way faulty. His beard is full, the same color as his hair; his eyes blue and extremely brilliant. In reproof and rebuke he is formidably; in exhortation and teaching, gentle and amiable of tongue. None have seen him to laugh, but many, on the contrary, to weep. His person is tall, his hands beautiful and straight. In speaking, deliberate, grave, little given to loquacity; in beauty surpassing most men.

---

8   Halley, Halley's Bible Handbook.

Miracles

From my childhood, I have been fascinated with the stories in the Bible and with the stories of the saints. It has always seemed to me that if these stories were true, I could put my full faith in the teachings of the Christian Church. Even more, I could believe that human beings are in a special relationship with God and that this relationship is sometimes marked by extraordinary outward characteristics and events.

Religiously, a miracle can be described as an extraordinary event manifesting a supernatural work of God. Scientifically, a miracle can be defined as an event not explainable by any known laws of nature.

MIRACLES OF THE OLD TESTAMENT

Noah

As we learn in the Old Testament, God performed many miracles for his chosen people. From Adam to Noah there was a lot of "begetting." Many of the generations of Adam lived to a ripe old age of nine hundred years, many fathering children past one hundred years of age. Noah fathered children at six hundred years old! So … it seems to me that there must have been a lot of people begotten very quickly.

Everyone knows the story of Noah and the ark. It is a story that I have found fascinating, because to me it speaks of God's ultimate frustration with his people and yet his forgiveness for some. God was unhappy with his people, because the earth was now filled with corruption and violence. The Jews were worshipping other Gods, so he decided to destroy all the creatures of the earth in 2400 BC with a great flood. Supposedly, the Mediterranean, Black Sea, and the Caspian Sea overflowed into the Persian Gulf, causing the flood. Noah, being a very devout follower, convinced God to spare him, his sons and their wives. Noah's sons went forth and populated all of Europe, Asia, and Africa. Shem propagated the Semites of Israel; Ham, the Hammites of Africa, Palestine, and Arabia; and Japheth, the Europeans and Asians.

In terms of objective evidence, Noah and the flood has arguably been the biblical story for which there has been the most rigorous search for such evidence. Berosus, a Babylonian historian of 300 BC, writing about the reign of the ancient kings of Babylon (Iraq), seemed to have modified the biblical story when he wrote that a certain king, Xisusthros, was warned by God to build a ship and take into it his relatives and every different animal and the necessary food. The ship was stranded in Armenia (the location of Mount Ararat). When the flood subsided, they sent out birds. The third time, they did not return. He then built a sacrificial altar. Many other cultures have legends of a great flood. Another similar story of the flood is told in the *Epic of Gilgamesh*, written before the time of Abraham, which states,

"The uproar of mankind is intolerable ... So the gods decided to exterminate mankind. They commanded, 'Tear down your house and build a boat—then take up into the boat all living creatures. I [Noah?] built six decks, below—divided them into nine sections with bulkheads between. I loaded into her all living things, my family, my kin, the beasts of field both wild and tame. The flood overwhelmed the world, but there appeared, a mountain [Ararat?] and there the boat grounded, I loosed a dove. She flew away but, finding no resting place, she returned. I made a sacrifice on the mountain top."

In his Bible handbook, Henry Halley states that the Egyptians, the Greeks, the Hindus. the Chinese, the English Druids, the Polynesians, the Mexicans, the Peruvians, the people of Greenland, and the American Indians all speak of a great flood that destroyed all mankind except one family.

Over the years, I have followed the stories of those seeking physical evidence of the Noah story very closely. I have looked forward to the day when I might see a piece of wood from the ark, settling for myself that the story literally occurred. In modern times, climbers have repeatedly claimed to have sighted Noah's ark on Mount Ararat as far back as the nineteenth century. Some reportedly climbed into the ark, and one even made a sketch showing the animal compartments.

In 1840, Turkish workmen stated that they saw the bow of a huge boat emerging from the ice on Mount Ararat. Geologists went to investigate and confirmed the find. They said that they were able to enter three chambers of the ark.

In 1893, Dr. Nouro of Jerusalem visited the site and said that he had found the bow and stern of the ark, but he was not able to enter because it was filled with snow.

In 1914, a Russian military pilot stated that he had seen the ark on the southern slope of Mount Ararat. The Russians sent 150 climbers to investigate his claim. They supposedly found the ark and photographed it. However, the photos and the report mysteriously vanished during the Bolshevik revolution of 1917.

In 1930, the English archeologist Sir Leonard Woolley was digging in an ancient burial ground in the city of Ur, which is located in the southern part of Iraq. As he dug down, he discovered layer after layer of artifacts that were the remains of the cities of different civilizations of the ancient past. As cities were destroyed by warfare, it was a practice to build the new city on the top of the old. The archeological excavations discovered a sedimentary deposit layer of a great flood, with no artifacts, in Babylon. The five to eight feet of sediment, with no artifacts, found above the relics of other ancient cities indicated a very great depth of water was there for a long period of time. Digs were made, covering nearly the entire country of modern-day Iraq. Woolley discovered that the entire country of Iraq was covered by the thick sediment layer, which showed that a great flood had extended way inland from the Persian gulf for hundreds of miles.[9]

Between 1952 and 1955, the French explorer Fernando Navarra reported that he had found the ark at 13,800 feet level on Mount Ararat, protruding from the ice. He stated that the boat was 450 feet long. This agrees remarkably with the Genesis account, which stated that the ark was ark was 300 cubits (450 feet). Could this be Noah's ark?

Several more expeditions to the site were made during the 1980s by joint American-Turkish explorers, who brought back samples of the ark, but no further tests have been reported. However, the director of the US expeditions believes that they

---

9   Rehwinkle, The Flood.

had found the ark site but no reason has ever been given regarding the study.

The Great Flood

Recently the Turkish government has refused access to Mount Ararat, so the only sightings have been by airplane and satellites. The heavy snowfall on the mountain now makes it difficult to locate the ark. Perhaps the recent global warming may eventually reveal further proof of its presence. But for now, it is based on hearsay and unsubstantiated claims by people who could not be considered objective—they wanted to find proof, and they claimed to have found it.

Henry Halley, in his Bible handbook theorizes that the rains were so heavy that the Mediterranean, the Caspian, and the Black Seas overflowed and poured into the Euphrates river valley (Iraq) and the Persian Gulf. Remains of several ancient cities have also been found several feet below the level of the Black Sea, which further corroborates this theory. At one time in the earth's history, geologists have discovered that most of Turkey, North Africa, and the Euphrates valley were beneath the Mediterranean, which makes Halley's theory of the great flood plausible. There is also speculation about a comet impact in the Arabian Sea that may have raised ocean levels at that time, which could have caused the flood.

Jonah and the Whale

Everybody has heard the story of Jonah being swallowed by a whale, but unless you read the Bible, you probably don't know why. God told Jonah to go to Nineveh and preach to the people there to repent. Nineveh was the capital of Assyria, the biggest enemy of Israel. He thought that it should have been God's duty to judge Nineveh for their wicked ways, so he boarded a ship and headed in the opposite direction. God was so furious with Jonah that he caused a terrible storm that was about to sink the boat. The sailors, realizing that Jonah was the problem, threw him overboard; and he was swallowed by a whale. Jonah prayed for three days while he was in the whale's belly, and when he promised to repent, the whale regurgitated him on the beach. God repeated again, "Go to Nineveh!" Jonah went. When Jonah arrived in Nineveh, he undoubtedly told them the story about his experience in the whale and probably told them that they would receive equal punishment if they did not repent and give up their evil ways. They believed him and no longer practiced their evil ways. Jonah was still unhappy that the people of Nineveh had gotten off so easy, so he complained to God again. God was so angry with Jonah that he caused a worm to kill Jonah's favorite shade tree, leaving Jonah to scorch in the sun. God gave Jonah a good scolding. A huge mound in Nineveh, one hundred feet high, bears Jonah's name. Supposedly, this was his burial place.

The Fertile Crescent

The lands surrounding Jordan River and the Tigris and Euphrates rivers contained some of the best agricultural land around the Mediterranean at that time. Because the rivers formed the shape of a sickle, it was known as the Fertile Crescent. After the development of farming, the people did not have to spend all of their time hunting wild game or forging for wild fruits and vegetables. With an available supply of water, cities and villages developed along the rivers. Canals were dug, and the land was turned into a lush green farmland. Thousands of years of overfarming have now turned the land into a semidesert. The people domesticated the wild sheep, pigs, and goats and planted the seeds of wild wheat, barley, emmer, and einkorn. The cities required a surplus of agricultural products to feed the growing populations. The canals were also essential for the trade and transportation as well as agriculture. Boats connected the villages along the canals. The Babylonian cities of Ur, Fara, Nippar, and Sippar developed along the Tigris and Euphrates rivers.

Jerusalem was located in the south central part of the land then known as Canaan. The Lebanon Mountains run down the eastern coast of the Mediterranean, and their snow-covered peaks supply water to the rivers flowing in the Jordan River Valley. The Orontes River flows north and supplied water for the ancient city of Antioch. The Abana River flows east and supplies water for the city Damascus. The Leontes River flows west and supplies the cities of Tyre and Siden with water. The Jordan River flows south and made Canaan the land of "milk and honey" promised to the Hebrews in the Bible. Jerusalem was built on five hills in the center of the mountain range between the Mediterranean on the west and the Jordan River to the east. Originally, it was located on the southeastern hill but was later expanded to include the other four hills. It was surrounded by deep valleys, which gave it excellent protection from marauding tribes. King David made Jerusalem the nation's capital in 1000 BC. The remains of an extensive fortification wall were found surrounding the city. As the city expanded, the wall was extended. The rivers flowing from the mountains provided fertile land for farming much the same as the Tigris and Euphrates rivers did in Babylon. Here again, the domestication of crops and animals and permanent city locations gave time for the development of crafts. The Sea of Galilee, made famous in the Bible, abounded with fish. The invention of pottery allowed for the storage of food and ease of transportation of wine. The invention of metal revolutionized agriculture with the invention of the plow and the production of tools and weapons. Here again, thousands of years of farming turned much of the land into a semidesert.[10]

Abraham

Of all the figures of the Old Testament, Abraham draws me. In him, I see a man who was so venerable that he is revered by Jews, Muslims, and Christians. The Babylonians then occupied the area now known as Iraq. They were a highly civilized culture that built many splendid cities. Abraham was a Semite, a distant relative

---

10   Karlowski and Sabloff, Ancient Civilizations.

of Shem, the son of Noah. By that time, Noah's generation had supposedly moved to Babylonia. Abraham was now living in Ur, on the Persian Gulf, 427 years after the flood.

The Babylonians

The city of Ur, where Abraham lived, contained one of the most important libraries of ancient times. The Code of Hammurabi was found there during archeological digs. Hammurabi was king of Babylonia at the time of Abraham. The laws covered everything from worship, justice, taxes, wages, interest, lending, property, dispute, marriage, partnerships, public works, canal building and care, passenger service and freight service by canal and camel caravans, to international commerce. Abraham must have been a very learned man, because Ur was profuse with schools and libraries, with thousands of books containing subjects on grammar, mathematics, astronomy, geography, religion, and politics. All of this knowledge was inscribed on clay tablets, which when baked became as hard as pottery. Abraham must have attended these schools and learned leadership, which was probably one of the reasons God chose him to lead his people.

At one time, Ur was one of the most important seaports in the world. Cargoes—mainly ore, copper, and building stones—were shipped down the Persian Gulf to seaports all over the ancient world. The remains of an ancient wall seventy feet thick and eighty feet high encircled the city. A sacred area was surrounded by an inner wall, which contained several temples and palaces. One of the most important discoveries were the royal tombs, which contained the remains of the queen, adored with a golden crown, beaded necklaces, and jewelry of gold and silver. With the queen, bones of forty court servants were found, which had been sacrificed.

Like the other ancient peoples of Babylon, the Jews were worshipping idols. When he was a youth, Abraham tried to convince his father, Terah, to stop worshipping idols and worship Abraham's one God. His father would not listen, so Abraham burned the shed storing the idols. God, seeing that he was a kindhearted, righteous, and God-fearing man, chose him to lead his people. God was not happy with his people, so he promised Abraham that he would become their patriarch if he would lead his people to the promised land of Palestine, which he did.

Abraham must have been a good military leader. When his nephew Lot was captured by the Babylonians, Abraham defeated the tribes of four of the Babylonian kings with only 318 of his best warriors and some local tribesman in a midnight raid and freed Lot. In 1929, the archeologist Albright discovered several huge mounds along the borders of Hauron, Gilead, and Moab, the remains of the cities that existed in 2000 BC that could have been the cities of the four eastern kings that once captured Lot.

When Abraham was eighty-six years old, his wife Sarah had not bore him any children, so she offered her slave girl, Hagar, to him so that he may have a son to continue his bloodline. Hagar bore him Ishmael. When Abraham was one hundred years old and Sarah was ninety years old, God promised that Sarah would bear him a son, and he would be called Isaiah. As Ishmael grew up, Sarah became worried that Ishmael, being the firstborn would inherit all of Abraham's herds, so she told Abraham that he should send Ishmael and his mother, Hagar, out into the wilderness. Abraham refused, but God told him that Ishmael would become the leader of the great nation (the Arab people), and so it came to pass. Isaiah became the leader of the Semites (Jews). His bloodline gave rise to Jacob, who fathered the leaders of the twelve tribes of Israel, including Judah, whose bloodline produced David, from whom Jesus is descended (see chart generations of Noah, Abraham, and David).

Abraham and his people lived in Palestine for two hundred years until a severe famine caused them to leave for Egypt, where they worked for four hundred years (whether or not as slaves is still being debated) and developed into a mighty culture (supposedly three million). However, God was again not happy with how his people were living, because they were starting to be influenced by the Egyptian worship of many gods, and he decided that they should return to Palestine and reestablish their nation.

What would it take for me to believe that Abraham actually lived and was, in fact, the forefather of both the Arabs and the Jews? As previously mentioned, after the flood, Noah's three sons, Japeth, Shem, and Ham, went out and resettled the earth. Shem's son's settled Israel, northern Arabia, and northern Iraq and Ham's sons, Phoenicia and Palestine (Canaan). Genetic evidence recently obtained by the National Geographic Society proves that indeed the Jews and the Palestinians have the same origin. The Canaanites (Arabs) broke away from the Israelites and began telling their own story to separate themselves from their Israelite cousins.

In his Bible handbook, Henry Halley states that there is archeological proof that Abraham visited Egypt around 2000 BC, because of famine in Egypt. On a tomb at Benihassen in Egypt, supposedly that of Pharaoh Senusert II of the Twelfth Dynasty, there is a carving depicting traders in Semite dresses arriving at the pharaoh's court. It must have been the visit of an important Semite leader in order to have been sculptured on a pharaoh's tomb. The most important Semite leader of that time was Abraham.[11]

11   Halley, Halley's Bible Handbook.

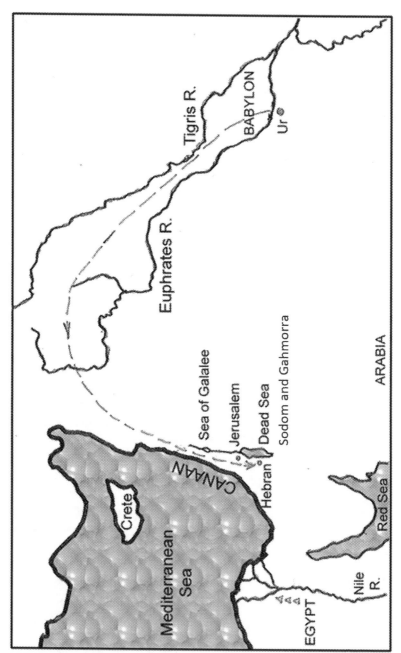

Abraham's Journey

In 1862, the Prince of Wales visited a cave at Machphelah in Palestine. He saw stone tombs carved with the names of Abraham, Isaiah, Jacob, Sarah, Rebekah, and Leah. Could this have been the family burial tomb of the family of Abraham?

Moses

Like most young Christians, I learned the story of Moses very early, and my most vivid memories were when Moses had been banished to the desert for killing an Egyptian. The angel of God appeared to him in the form of a burning bush and told him to lead his people out of Egypt. Pharaoh Ramses II refused to let the Hebrews go, so God threatened him with ten plagues of monumental proportion.

First, the Nile River was turned blood red, killing all the fish. Second, Egypt was overrun by frogs. Third and fourth, Egypt was plagued with lice and flies. Fifth, the Egyptian cattle and horses died. Sixth, the people were inflicted with boils. Seventh, hail and fire fell from the skies. Eighth, locusts devoured their crops. Ninth, the sun did not appear for three days.

After each of these, the pharaoh was not convinced, so God inflicted a final plague on Egypt, causing the death of all the firstborn of Egypt, including the pharaoh's son. Pharaoh agreed to let the Hebrews go, so they packed their belongings and headed out into the desert. Inscriptions found in the Pharaoh's tomb indicate that the death of his firstborn could not be explained. In 1912, Egyptian inscriptions found by Sir Flinders Petrie in a tomb erected in the Seventeenth Dynasty confirms that the Jews were in Egypt and the Exodus at the time. In 1905, he found a slab of black stone in Egypt, which reads, "Plundered is Canaan (Palestine). Israel is desolated; his seed is not. Palestine has become a widow for Egypt." This sounds like Joshua's conquest of Palestine during the Exodus. In 1922, excavations sponsored by the University Museum of Pennsylvania found a stele commissioned by Pharaoh Ramses II at Bethshan in Palestine, stating he "built [the city of] Ramses with the Asiatic Semitic slaves." This is further proof that the Israelis were slaves in Egypt.

Burgsh, in his book *Egypt under the Pharaohs*, describes an Egyptian inscription he found in a rock-cut tomb, which confirms the biblical account of the seven years of famine in Egypt.

The ancient Roman historian Josephus wrote that Moses commanded an army of Egyptians before his banishment to the desert. This offers further proof other than the Bible that Moses existed.

In recent years, scientists have offered explanations for some of the plagues of Egypt that do not rely on divine intervention. For instance, there is a strain of algae that turns water red and is highly toxic to aquatic life. Perhaps this toxin drove the frogs away from the Nile and into the villages. Lice and flies bred in the dead fish. These insects bit the cattle, infecting them with blood-borne diseases. One of these diseases was also transmitted to humans, leading to boils and to infant death. Being somewhat scientific in my world view by nature, I find these alternative explanations plausible, but I still feel that there is something miraculous in this story that is not easily explained.

Exodus

I come from an immigrant family. When my ancestors came from Italy, they came with a faith in the possibility of a better life and very little else. Although they may not have used the term "miracle," they did pray that they would find what they needed for the long journey when they arrived. For that reason, the story of Exodus resonates for me.

According to the biblical account, what followed was a series of miracles unparalleled in human history:

1. Departure from Egypt in 1400 BC.

2. Then the Red Sea was parted for the Hebrews but swallowed the Egyptians in pursuit. A cover of clouds gave them shade and guided them by day and a pillar of fire at night.

3. Seeds dropped from heaven each morning and were used for making unleavened bread (manna) and quail came out of nowhere and provided food.

4. Water appeared from rocks, twice, when they ran out of water.

5. God caused the Ten Commandments to be cut into rock tablets at Mount Sinai. The earth shook, and the mountain exploded with terrifying flames.

6. After Moses had spent time with God on Mount Sinai, his face shone with such brilliance that he had to wear a veil so that he would not blind people. Scientific investigation indicates that Mount Sinai had been volcanic sometime in the past, which would corroborate the story that the fire shot out of the mountain when Moses spoke to God.

7. Along the way, the Israelites had to fight off the fierce desert tribes that blocked their way. The remains of many fortified cities have been found, which corroborates their path. After two years in the desert, they reached the Palestinian border at Kadesh, and the Hebrews sent spies to determine if it would be possible to defeat the Canaanites.

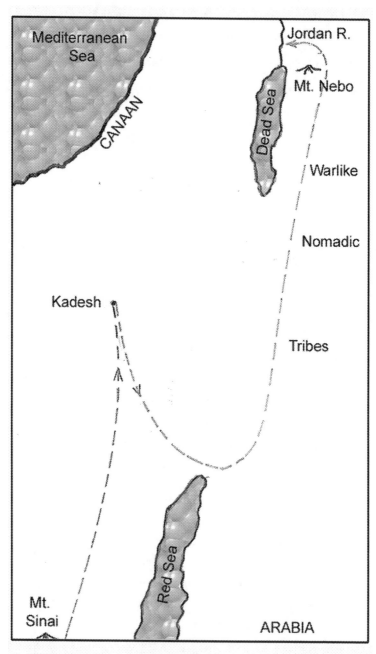

Exodus

They were overwhelmed with fear and refused to enter. Because of their lack of faith, God sent them back to the desert, where they roamed for another thirty-eight years until they reached the Jordan River. At Kadash (now Ain Kadees), a large Oasis has been found with streams flowing beneath a rock. Could this have been the rock that Moses had struck, producing water?

Some of these plagues and miracles could be explained by scientists as natural acts, but the fact that they appeared in succession and were witnessed by thousands flies in the face of coincidence.

In his book *Archaeological Proof of the Exodus*, the noted author Sydney Yackovovich claims that there is written proof that the Jews were in Egypt circa 1700 to 1500 BC. The pharaoh Atmose commissioned a stele (monument), circa 1500 BC, which reads a lot like the conditions that existed during the Hebrews' stay in Egypt. He believes that the Hyksos, a band of warlike shepherds related to the Hebrews, went to Egypt circa 1700 BC and conquered Egypt. Their capital was at Avarus, according to the stele. After the Hyksos were expelled by the pharaoh Atmuse, the Hebrews that remained were reduced to slavery. It further states that there was a great storm and complete darkness in Egypt at that time. According to a papyrus found at Avarus, the Egyptians were pelted with hail and fire from the sky. Surprisingly, a cemetery was found in Egypt showing graves of only male children. This corroborates the Bible story "that all the firstborn of Egypt would die" (Exod. 11, 12). The mummy of one pharaoh showed that he had died at the young age of twelve. The remains of an ancient spring found on the top of Mount Sinai confirm that Moses could have gotten water from the rocks.

Joshua

The Bible goes on to tell the story of Joshua. God then offered the Hebrews a second chance to win Palestine. This time God had given them Joshua, a brilliant military leader. With God's help, they won all of their battles against the Canaanites.

1. First, the Ark of the Covenant caused the river Jordan to dry up so Joshua's army could cross to Jericho.

2. Then the ark flew before them with a terrifying wailing, and the Canaanites fled in fear, the walls of the fortress of Jericho came tumbling down, and the Hebrews captured the city. Dr. John Garstrong, director of the British School of Archeology, Jerusalem, excavated Jericho and found that the city had been destroyed by a fire at the time of Joshua, and the fortress wall did indeed fall flat.

3. The Canaanites were pelted with huge hailstones. The cities of Ai and Bethel were destroyed.

4. Joshua read the book of Laws to the people at Mount Ebal.

5. At Gibeon, the sun remained in the sky for more than a day so Joshua could win the battle.

6. The cities of Lachish, Megiddo, and Hazor were destroyed by fire. Recently, archeological excavations show that these cities were in fact destroyed by fire at that time.

Here again, these miracles were witnessed by thousands and could not be mere coincidences.

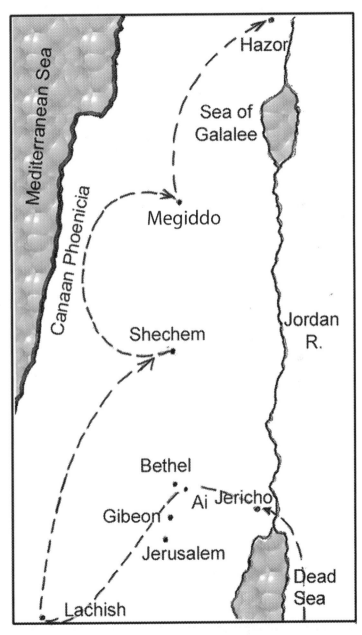

Joshua's Conquests

After Joshua conquered the Canaanites, the Hebrews called their new country Israel; they soon encountered the Canaanite religion, which worshipped the gods of fertility, Baal and Astarte. Newlywed Canaanite women had to engage in intercourse with men other than their husband on the eve of their marriage. Also, Canaanite maidens sold themselves for sex, and payment went to the temple treasuries. This was quite a shock for the simple shepherd people, whose religion was so strict and puritanical. Joshua ruled Israel until his death. After the Hebrews were settled into their new country, they were ruled by wise men called judges for three hundred years. They then decided that they should have a king like all the other nations. The first king of Israel, Saul, was appointed because of his decisive battles against the Philistines, a highly militaristic culture that controlled the coast of Canaan. It was a Philistine maiden, Delilah, who deceived Sampson into cutting his hair. Samson had been appointed by God to free Israel from the Philistines. God gave him superhuman strength for this purpose. When Samson became infatuated with Delilah, he revealed the secret that his strength lay in his long hair. She used this secret to cause his demise.

These were such monumental events; it seemed to me that there should be nonbiblical sources to corroborate the stories. There is some objective proof. Letters found from Armana in Palestine written to Pharaoh Amenhotep urgently requested help, because Palestine was being lost to the Habiri (Hebrews). They were destroying the Canaanite cities and plundering the countryside. This sounds remarkably like Joshua's conquest of Palestine in the Bible. Archeological evidence in Palestine has revealed the remains of several fortified hilltop cities that had existed during the time of Moses, which showed signs of burning.

All of this seems to confirm the books in the Bible. Also, Joshua's name appears in the Armani tablets.

David

From my childhood, I remember the story of how David slew the giant warrior Goliath, but David had a gentler side and wrote beautiful poetry, like the twenty-third Psalm.

The giant Goliath, whom David slew, was a Philistine. King Saul, who ruled at the time, was eventually killed in a battle with the Philistines, and the kingdom was then ruled by David. David finally defeated the Philistines, and the twelve tribes of Israel were united under a single nation.

David's bloodline can be traced back to Abraham. David's lineage produced Joseph, the father of Jesus. David ruled over Israel for forty years and made it a mighty kingdom. After his affair with Bathsheba, his grief nearly broke him, as did other sad events. His daughter was raped by her brother Amnon. Amnon was murdered by his brother Absalom. Absalom led the revolt against his father and was killed in battle. David had violated another man's wife. As a result, David's wives were raped in public. God eventually forgave David, because of his unfailing trust and his endless gratitude to his God.

The watercourse that David's men used to enter the city of Jerusalem and capture the city was discovered in 1886 by the archeologist Warren. It is a sloping tunnel with the steps cut through solid rock, which supplied water to the city and passed beneath the twenty-four-foot-thick wall, which surrounded the city. Without the passage, the city would have been impregnable. The remains of the wall, which was four hundred feet long, have been uncovered. It was built in the time of King David and is known as David's Wall. The remains of the foundation of the older wall can be seen under David's Wall. This corroborates the Bible's story that David was the king of Jerusalem at the time.

Solomon

I remember King Solomon for making Jerusalem one of the most beautiful cities in the world at the time, but the cost had a more sinister side.

Jerusalem is located in the land of Israel, about forty miles east of the Mediterranean, in a valley surrounded by two mountain ranges. To the east the Jordan River flows. It is located on five hilltops. Originally, the city stood on the southeast hill, because there was a spring at its base, which furnished water to the city. In ancient times, cities were built on hilltops and surrounded by walls, which furnished protection from invading tribes. By Jesus's time, the city was expanded to the north and west to include all five hilltops.

After David's death, David's son Solomon took over the throne and built the great temple, a wall of which still remains (the Wailing Wall of the Jews). Solomon's temple was built with huge blocks of stone fifteen feet in length, with rafters of cedar, and the inside was overlain with gold and silver. The east entrance was supported by pillars of brass thirty-five feet high. The altar supposedly stood on the rock (Dome of the Rock) where Abraham offered Isaiah as a sacrifice to God. To the south, a huge brass tank, fifteen feet in diameter, supported by twelve brass oxen contained the water with which the priests purified themselves after the sacrifices. Solomon's palace stood to the south of the temple and was much grander. Remains of the original city wall, four hundred feet long and seventy-five feet high in some places, has been excavated. Many of the vessels were of gold, and Solomon's throne was of ivory overlain with gold.

King Solomon also had a great navy. He conquered the Phoenician navy at Tyre and used it for trade on the Mediterranean. He had a major seaport at Eflon-geber, south of Jerusalem, on the Gulf of Akaba, which had access to the Red Sea, Arabia, India, and Africa. Through this commerce, he built Israel into one of the most powerful nations at that time. Ruins of this seaport were found in 1939 by the American School of Oriental Research. The remains of metal smelting furnaces and refineries were found there along with dishes, nails, spearheads, and fishhooks.

At Megiddo in Israel, the remains of a huge stable were found, which housed hundreds of Solomon's horses. Hitching posts and mangers were found there, indicating that it had been a stable.

King Solomon asked for wisdom to govern his people fairly, and God gave it to him, because it was a sincere request. He was known as an intellectual wonder of the ancient world. He excelled as a scientist, botanist, zoologist, political ruler, successful business man, poet, and preacher. Kings and scholars came from around the ancient world to hear his lectures. Solomon was a wise leader at first. What happened later plunged the country into financial disaster. He bankrupted his people with excessive taxation in order to rebuild Israel. When Solomon's building projects were completed, the laborers became the idle poor. Solomon married many Canaanite women (a total of seven hundred) and started to worship their false idols, which was a direct insult to God. After Solomon's death, civil war broke out, and Israel was divided into two kingdoms—one to the north, Judah, and one to the south, Israel. Israel was ruled by many kings after Solomon's death.

The most infamous of these kings was King Ahab and his wife, the promiscuous Jezebel, who proceeded to provoke God's anger by worshiping the Canaanite false gods. Jezebel was determined to rid Jerusalem of the Jews' worship of their God. She was a devoted worshiper of the Canaanite god, Baal, and had a temple built for him, employed 850 priests to spread this heathen religion, had the Israeli prophets of God killed, and abolished the Jewish religion. But her rule was soon to be brought to an end. God had entrusted the prophet Elijah with the sole purpose of destroying the idol worship of Baal. The Baal religion included the sacrifice of children. The remains of several children were found buried in pottery jars in a cemetery next to the temple devoted to Ashtoreth, the goddess of Baal. This is proof that the worshipers of Baal did indeed murder little children as part of their religion. Elijah was determined to rid Jerusalem of this wicked religion. First, he declared that God would cause severe drought. After three and half years of drought, Jezebel would not change her wicked ways. Then he threatened that God would send fire and flood down upon her, but that still did not convince Jezebel. Finally, he decided that he would trick the priests of Baal to end the wicked religion.

Elijah challenged their priests to a showdown (the flaming altar miracle). The prophets of Baal prayed to their gods, but no fire appeared on their altar. Elijah dowsed his altar with water and prayed to God. Fire shot down from heaven and consumed the sacrifice, the water, and the altar! Much to their dismay, the priests of Baal were driven out of town and killed. Elijah still did not think he had fulfilled his duty, so he asked God to take his life. However, Elijah did not die; instead, God had him taken to heaven in a chariot pulled by angels.

The Ark of the Covenant

The ark is very significant to me, because it housed the stones on which the Ten Commandments had been inscribed by God, which was then given to Moses on Mount Sinai. The Bible describes the ark in vivid detail. It was made of acacia wood overlaid with gold. The lid was made of solid gold, with two cherubs with outstretched wings facing each other. Many miracles were attributed to the ark. As previously mentioned, during Joshua's battle at Jericho, the ark caused the waters of the River Jordan to stop flowing so that Joshua could pursue his enemy. God caused the walls of Jericho to "fall flat" instead of crumbling. Archeological evidence confirms this. The ark then flew before him into battle, howling like a banshee, scaring the enemy so badly that they retreated. It is recorded that only the high priests of the Jews were allowed to touch it for fear of death. One of the carriers of the ark stumbled and tried to steady the ark and was immediately killed. When the ark was stolen by the Philistines, they were infected with a plague so bad that they returned it in seven months.

In order to test the power of the ark, the National Geographic Society provided funding for an exact replica to be built. Indeed, it acted like a huge electrical capacitor, storing the electrical charge placed on it and discharging it when touched. It was not enough electricity to harm someone, but who knows what would happen if a high electrical charge, such as lightning, had been applied to it?

Ethiopian legends indicate that during this period, the queen of Sheba traveled to Israel and fell in love with King Solomon. When she returned to Ethiopia, she had his son, Menelik I.

When Menelik grew older, he reportedly stole the ark from

Israel and brought it to Ethiopia. The ark is now being kept under guard at St. Mary of Zion church in Aksum on the northern Ethiopian border. No one but a sacred monk has access to the ark. Supposedly, anyone else who looked at the ark would die. However, since no one else had seen the ark, this fable cannot be corroborated. This story has overtones of the Bible, which states that anyone, other than the high priests of Israel, who touched the ark would die.[12]

Sodom and Gomorrah

I believe that God destroyed Sodom and Gomorrah as an example to future generations of what could happen if they continue to practice their evil ways. According to the Bible, God was very unhappy with the people of Sodom and Gomorrah, because the people were performing unspeakable wickedness, so he was intent on destroying them. Lot pleaded with him not to destroy the city, because there were still some good people there. God bargained with him that if he could identify even one good person he would not destroy the cities. Because Lot was not able to find one good person, God destroyed them by raining fire and brimstone on the cities. God warned Lot and his family to leave the city and not to turn around. Lot's wife ignored the warning and was immediately turned to a pillar of salt. Indeed, one of the pillars of salt found at the south end of the Dead Sea bears her name.

In 1924, an archeological expedition found the remains of a walled city (Babedra) at the southeast end of the Dead Sea, dating to about 2500 to 2000 BC, which had been destroyed suddenly. The area around the Dead Sea contains great quantities of bitumen, asphalt, pitch, and brimstone (sulfur)—the ingredients

---

12 Smithsonian, December 2007.

of gun powder. Henry Halley, in his Bible handbook, theorizes that God ignited the asphalt and brimstone, causing a tremendous explosion. This would indeed cause fire and brimstone to fall from the sky, destroying both cities. In 1973, an archeological expedition found the remains of another city (Numera), which had been completely destroyed at the same time as Babedra. Hundreds of skeletal remains that had not been buried in a graveyard were found. Could these be the citizens of Sodom and Gomorrah?

The Tower of Babel

One hundred years after the great flood (2300 BC), God realized that Babylon was getting overcrowded, so he caused the people to start speaking in different tongues, knowing that if they did not understand each other, they would leave to start populating the rest of the world. This occurred in the city of Babylon, where a huge tower was being constructed—the Tower of Babel (Gen. 11:1–9).

An ancient tablet was found there, stating that "the building of the illustrious tower offended the gods. They [the gods] threw down what they had built, scattered them abroad, and made strange their speech." An immense foundation hole, 330 feet on each side and full of bricks, has been found there. The tower must have been of considerable height, resembling the stepped pyramids found in Egypt. This provides both written and archeological proof of the Bible.

The Hanging Gardens of Babylon

Remains of the Hanging Gardens of Babylon have been found in the city of Babylon. Remains of a wall that was fifteen miles on each side and eighty feet thick has been found there. The city was profuse with temples and immense golden statues. What once was Nebuchadnezzar's palace has also been found there. It was one of the most magnificent buildings ever constructed. The Hanging Gardens of Babylon were one of the seven wonders of the ancient world. They were built for Nebuchadnezzar's beautiful queen. Several tiers of arches, four hundred feet square, were covered with flowers and trees. Water for the gardens was delivered by pumps from the Euphrates River to the top of the roof. Beneath the arches were luxurious apartments.

The Fall of Israel

I believe that God let Israel be destroyed, because he felt that the people were no longer faithful to him.

After this, God tried to call his people back to him, but it was a futile effort. Assyrian and Babylonian inscriptions found at Nineveh and Lacish indicate that the northern kingdom fell to the Assyrian's King Sargon in 720 BC, and the southern kingdom fell to the Babylonian's King Nebuchadnezzar in 600 BC. The Israelites were carried into slavery; God did nothing to help.

The Assyrians possessed the greatest fighting machine of their time. They even had siege towers with wheels, which could be rolled up to the city wall; warriors could then enter a city and conquer it. They were the cruelest warriors of the ancient world. Records found on clay tablets state that they would skin some of the prisoners alive, cut off their hands, feet, noses, ears, pull out their eyes, pull out their tongues, and even make piles of human skulls. Hundreds of thousands of Israelites were captured and sent to other lands. Israel ceased to exist as an independent nation. Layers of ashes were unearthed from the fires set dating back to 600 BC, as well as temple treasures, an altar, sacrificed bones, and food supplies, corroborating that the burning was sudden.

In 600 BC to 591 BC, the Babylonian king Nebuchadnezzar had all of the temple treasures of Jerusalem sent to Babylon. Jerusalem was burned and the city walls were torn down. The king of Israel, Zedekiah, was blinded; and thousands of city officials were sent to Babylon so that there was no longer any city government. Jerusalem was such a fortified city that it took the Babylonians one and half years to conquer it after having besieged it for eleven years.

Persian inscriptions indicate that it was not until King Cyrus of Persia captured Jerusalem (540 BC) that the Jews were allowed to return and rebuild the temple and, by 445 BC, rebuild the walls around Jerusalem. From this time forth Israel was not an independent nation, being ruled first by the Greeks (330 BC) and then the Syrians (175 BC).[13]

Ancient Roman historians Josephus and Eusebius record that the Jews made one last attempt to regain power in 164 BC, led by the military family of Maccabees, but this lasted for only one hundred years. When the Maccabees were fighting amongst themselves in 63 BC, the Romans stepped in to end the squabble, declared Israel a Roman province, and appointed the infamous King Herod to rule it.

In AD 70, the Jewish Zealot faction started another revolt, but they were finally defeated by the Romans at the Battle of Masada. The Romans leveled Jerusalem, and the Jews were forbidden to enter the city. Many of them were scattered all over the Mediterranean and Europe. The Canaanites (Palestinians) eventually regained control of Israel after the fall of the Roman Empire and named it Palestine.

13   Halley, Halley's Bible Handbook.

The Jews were driven out of many countries in the Middle Ages during the Spanish Inquisitions. God's final insult to the Jews was when he allowed 5 million of them to be executed during the World War II holocaust.

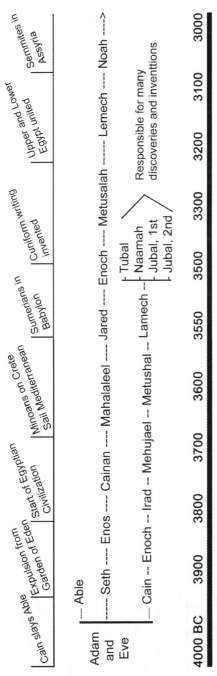

The Generations of Adam and Eve

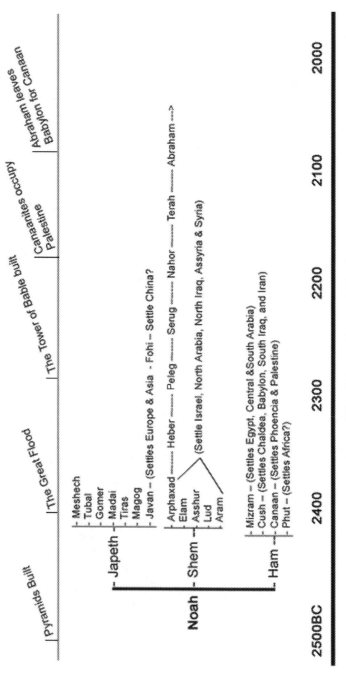

The Generations of Noah

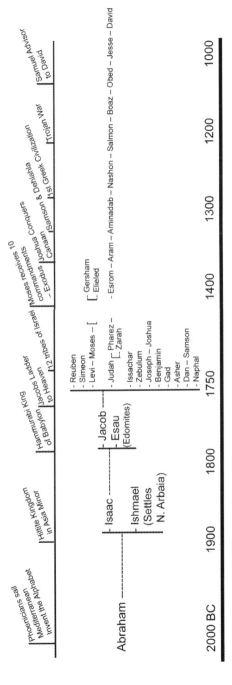

The Generations of Abraham

| 2000 BC | 1900 | 1800 | 1750 | 1400 | 1300 | 1200 | 1000 |

Phoenicians sail Mediterranean Invent the Alphabet

Hittite Kingdom in Asia Minor

Hammurabi King of Babylon

Jacobs Ladder to Heaven

12 tribes of Israel

Moses receives 10 commandments Joshua Conquers

Exodus Joshua Canaan

Samson & Dehlahla
1st Greek Civilization

Canaan Samson Trojan War

Samuel Advisor to David

Abraham

Isaac

Ishmael (Settles N. Arbaia)

Jacob
Esau (Edomites)

- Reuben
- Simeon
- Levi — Moses —
- Judah ⌐ Pharez –
         ⌊ Zarah
- Issachar
- Zebulum
- Joseph – Joshua
- Benjamin
- Gad
- Asher
- Dan – Samson
- Naphal

⌐ Gersham
⌊ Elieled

- Esrom – Aram – Aminadab – Nashon – Salmon – Boaz – Obed – Jesse – David

1000 BC	David	Saul 1st King of Israel
	Soloman	David slays Goliath – Succeeds Saul
	Rehoboam	Solomon builds his temple – Succeeds David
900 BC	Abijah	Phoenicians sail Mediterranean
	Asa	Egypt pillages Jerusalem
	Jehoshaphat	Elijah rides chariots of fire to Heaven
800 BC	Jehoram	Jonah survives whale
	Ozziah	Etruscan civilization in Italy
	Jutham	Isaiah predicts birth of Jesus
	Ahaz	City of Rome founded
700 BC	Hezikiah	North Israel falls to Assyrians
	Manasseh	End of the Assyrian Empire
600 BC	Amon	South Israel falls to Babylonians
	Josiah	Ezekiel sees the face of God
	Jeconiah	Daniel survives the lion's den
	Salathiel	Nebuchadnezzar burns Jerusalem
500 BC	Zerrubrabel	Etruscans defeat Romans
	Abiud	Persians rule Israel
400 BC	Eliakim	Gauls capture city of Rome
	Azor	Alexander the Great conquers Israel
300 BC	Sadoc	End of the Babylonia Empire
	Achim	Hannibal attacks Rome
200 BC	Eliuid	Maccabees rule Israel
	Eleazar	Greece under Roman rule
100 BC	Matthan	Julius Ceasar dictator of Rome
	Jacob	Rome conquers Israel - Herod King of Israel
6 AD	Joseph	Birth of Jesus
35 AD	Jesus	Crucifixion, Resurrection & Ascension

The Generations of David

MIRACLES OF THE NEW TESTAMENT

The Ministries of Jesus

The coming of Jesus was predicted by many of the Old Testament prophets. However, the Jews expected the Messiah to be a great military leader, who would drive the Romans out of Israel much the same as God had saved them in the past. They would not accept Jesus as the Messiah, because of his pacifist approach. After the crucifixion of Jesus, God seemed to have stopped protecting the Jews as he did in the past, when they were practicing idolatry instead of believing in him.

Christians have longed for proof that Jesus actually lived. In the face of life's many challenges, including the inevitable fate of death, it would be extremely comforting to have proof that the son of God actually came to Earth, had sympathy for the human plight, and could ultimately save us from death. But the objective proof of Jesus's birth and miraculous acts has been elusive.

The Scriptures tell us little about the early life of Jesus— his birth, the visit from the Wise Men, his escape into Egypt, his circumcision according to Jewish ritual, and his return to Nazareth after the death of Herod. However, there is one very important passage from Luke 2:41–52 that tells us that Jesus knew that he was the son of God at the age of twelve. After attending the feast of the Passover in Jerusalem, his family was returning to Nazareth when they discovered that Jesus was missing. When they returned to Jerusalem they found him in the temple, in the midst of the Pharisees, astounding them with his knowledge of the Holy Scriptures. He asked his parents, "Why are you looking for me? Did you not know that I had to be about my father's house?" He was referring to the temple as the house of God.

Why is there no record of Jesus for the next twenty years? The Bible states that "after this, he went down to Nazareth with them, and he continued in subjection to them." In other words, he became a carpenter's apprentice to Joseph and continued his study of the Scriptures. He performed no miracles and gave no sermons, so there was nothing to draw the attention of the scribes to write about.

The prophet Edgar Cayce does give us a glimpse of Jesus's early childhood in some of his psychic readings. The following are in the Cayce Library:

The family spent four and a half years at Alexandria, Egypt, after their escape from Herod's soldiers. They then returned to Jerusalem, where Jesus remained until the age of twelve and was educated in Jewish law and Scripture. The family then traveled to Judea and Capernaum. Jesus returned to Egypt for two and a half years and then went to India and Persia, where he studied astrology until the age of sixteen. He then returned to Egypt for five years, where he studied mysticism and prepared for priesthood. There, Jesus was also taught how each soul was reincarnated until it reached fulfillment. Egypt was the center of knowledge for the entire known world at the time. The family then returned to Capernaum, where Jesus was schooled as a minister and as a teacher.[14]

However, after, he was baptized by John at the age of thirty-two (Matt. 3:13–17). "Heaven was opened" and a voice came out of heaven, saying, "Thou art my beloved son in whom I am well pleased" he then realized his calling and went to cleanse himself in the desert for forty days. Satan then knew the power

14 Cayce, The Story of Jesus.

of God and tried to tempt Jesus so that he would reject God and worship him, offering him all the kingdoms of the world. After he admonished the devil, the angels came and ministered to him, for he was weak with hunger.

The ministry of Jesus began when he was approached by his first disciples (John, Andrew, Simon Peter, Philip, and Nathanael), who recognized he was indeed the son of God (John 1:35–51). They followed him to Galilee, where he performed his first miracle at Cana, turning the water to wine at the marriage feast. Here he addressed his mother, brusquely saying, "Woman, what have I to do with thee?" Here again, as in the temple when he was twelve, he did not recognize her as his mother but replied like he was the son of God (John 2:1–12).

Returning to Jerusalem, he cleansed the temple for the first time, driving out the sellers of livestock and the money changers, showing his aggressive side for the first time. One other time, he again cleansed the temple in Jerusalem. According to John 2:13 to 4:3, Jesus spent the first eight months of his ministry in Judah, giving sermons by the Jordan River. Then he left for Nazareth. On his way, he received water from a Samaritan woman at Jacob's well, which was strictly against the Jewish religion. The well remains to this day.

Returning to Nazareth, he so enraged the crowd with his controversial teaching that they took him to a hill to throw him over. Narrowly escaping death, he went to Capernaum, where his sermons were better accepted (Luke 4:16–30).

He resided two years at Galilee, where most of his miracles were performed—i.e., the miracle of the fishes, the Sermon on the Mount, the calming of the seas of Galilee, the healing of demoniacs, the feeding of five thousand people with two fishes and a few loaves of bread, walking on water, and countless cures

(Matt. 4:12, 19:1; Mark 1:14,10:1; Luke 4:14, 9:51). After his transfiguration on Mount Herman, he resided in Perea, northeast of Jerusalem, where he spent four months ministering (Matt. 19, 20; Mark 10; Luke 9:15, 19:29; John 7–11).

Returning to Jerusalem, he raised Lazarus from the dead, and then Jesus cleansed the temple for the second time, which infuriated the Pharisees (Matt. 21:12–17; Mark 11:15–19; Luke 19:45–48). When he made his triumphal entry into Jerusalem on Palm Sunday (Matt. 21:1–9; Mark 11:1–10; Luke 19:28–44; John 12:12–16), the Pharisees feared that he was gaining too much power and would cause a riot. Should this have happened, it would have upset the Roman ruler, and the Pharisees would be removed from office. So they concocted a false claim of treason against Jesus. The Romans believed the claim to be true and had him crucified. He was pierced on his side to make sure he was dead. Suddenly, darkness covered the earth, the veil in the temple was torn top to bottom, the tombs were opened, and the earth shook. As prophesized in the Old Testament, Jesus rose from the dead on the third day (Easter Sunday).

Jesus remained on Earth forty days after his resurrection. He appeared to the apostles at least eleven times through closed doors, after which he passed into the clouds on the hilltops above Bethany. He promised he would return in the clouds, visible for the entire world to see.

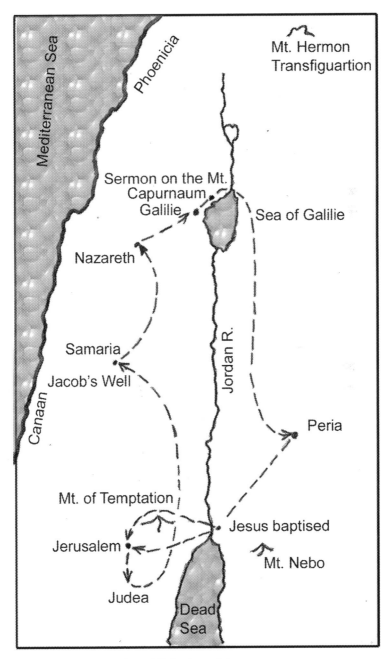

The Ministries of Jesus

Prophecies of the Bible

Several of the prophets of the Old Testament predicted the coming
of the Messiah (Savior):

- That he would be of the family of David (Sam.
  7:12–16; Ps. 89:3–4, 110:1, 132:11; Isa. 7:14)

- That he would be born of a virgin (Isa. 7:14)

- That he would be born in Bethlehem (Mal. 5:2)

- That he would reside in Galilee (Isa. 9:1, 2)

- That his coming would be announced by a herald
  angel (Isa. 40:3–5; Mal. 3:1, 4:5)

- His coming would cause the massacre of
  Bethlehem's children (Gen. 35:19–20, Jer. 31:15)

- His ministry would be one of healing (Isa. 53:4)

- That he would teach in parables (Isa., Ps. 78:2)

- That he would be disbelieved and rejected by the
  rulers (Ps. 69:4, 118:22; Isa. 6:10, 29:13,53:1)

- That he would make a triumphal entry into
  Jerusalem (Isa. 62:11, Zech. 9:9, Ps. 118:26)

- That he would be betrayed for thirty pieces of silver
  (Zech. 11:12, Ps. 41:9)

- That he would die with criminals (Isa. 53:9)

- That he would be buried by a rich man (Isa. 53:9)

- That he would be given vinegar and gall (Ps.
  69:21)

- That they would cast lots for his garments (Ps.
  22:18)

- His side would be pierced (Zech. 12:10, Ps. 12:16)

- He would rise from the dead on the third day (Ps. 12:16)

- That his rejection would be followed by the destruction of Jerusalem (Dan. 9:27; 11:31; 12:1,11)

The prediction of all these events long before they occurred goes way beyond the laws of probability and confirms that indeed Jesus was the Messiah and the Son of God.

Miracles of Jesus

Jesus performed many miracles during his short time on earth. The most notable of these was his resurrection from the dead, his transfiguration, and his accession into heaven. The next day after his death, Mary Magdalene went to anoint his body with precious oils, which was the Jewish rite after death. Finding his body missing, she wept. At which time, an angel appeared to her and told her that Jesus has risen from the dead. Later, as she left the tomb, she encountered a person whom she did not recognize. This was because Jesus's body had been transfigured to what he looked like when he was a young man. In that period of history, thirty-two was considered middle-aged. However, when he spoke she recognized his voice immediately. Jesus spent his last days preaching to his apostles, after which he ascended into heaven before their eyes.

Jesus performed many other miracles during his ministry. He healed the sick and cured the deaf, dumb, blind, crippled, and the lepers. As he preached from city to city, these miracles were witnessed by multitudes. He raised Lazarus, Jabirus's daughter and the widow's son from the dead. He cast out the evil spirits of many demoniacs. Although they were not as spectacular as the miracles in the Old Testament, Jesus also performed miracles over nature. He turned water to wine at a wedding, stilled the waters of the Sea of Galilee, twice caused Peter and his fishermen to fill their nets with fish, and even walked on water and fed over five thousand with a few fish and loaves of bread during his sermons. Here again, these miracles were witnessed by thousands and confirms that Jesus must have been the Son of God.

Did Jesus really exist? Were there any dependable, more objective histories written at the time that mention Jesus? Aside from the Bible, *Halley's Bible Handbook* cites that the first-century historian Josephus wrote a description of Jesus's life and resurrection shortly after the death of Christ.

> *About this time there lived one Jesus, a wise man, if indeed one should call him a man. For he was one who wrought surprising feats and was a teacher of such people as accept the truth gladly. He won over many Jews and many of the Greeks. This man was the Christ.*
>
> *When Pilate, upon hearing him accused of treason by men of the highest standing amongst them, he condemned him to be crucified. Those who had in the first place come to love him did not give up their affection for him.*
>
> *On the third day he appeared to them living, for the prophets of God had prophesied these and countless other marvelous things about him. And the tribe of the Christians, so-called after him, have still to this day not disappeared.*

In *Antiquities of the Jews*, Josephus, the Roman historian, cites references to Jesus Christ, John the Baptist, and James, the brother of Jesus. He mentions the Roman tax census that took place shortly after King Herods's rule. The gospel of Luke corroborates that Jesus was born at this time. Josephus mentions the death of John the Baptist at the request of Herod Antipas. Josephus goes on to describe the stoning death of James, the brother of Jesus, and calls Jesus the Messiah.

The Roman historian Suetonius, in *The Lives of the Twelve Caesars*, states that the Jews were expelled from Rome by the Emperor Claudius for making disturbances instigated by one Chrestus (Christ). The expulsion is also mentioned in Acts 18–2 of the Bible. He goes on to describe the persecution of the Christians in AD 64, who were blamed for the burning of Rome caused by Nero.

The Greek historian Eusebius (AD 260–340), in his *Church History*, describes the events that happened to the Jews after the crucifixion of Jesus. He describes the deaths of the apostles, St Peter and St. Paul, and the persecutions of the Christians by the Romans up to this time. Eusubius links Christ with the prophecies of the Old Testament. He further goes on to describe the stoning of James. The people said, "Let us stone James." While they pelted him, a priest called out, "Stop what you are doing." Then one of them, seeing he was still alive, clubbed him to death. He also goes on to say that the revolt in Judea was the result of James's death.

The anti-Christian scholar Celsus, writing shortly after the death of Christ, nevertheless agrees that Jesus came from a village in Judea (Bethlehem?), that he was the son of a Jewish mother and a carpenter father (no names given), and describes him as having magical powers.

Another ancient scholar, Tertullian, writing of how the Jews perceived Jesus, stated that Jesus was the son of a Jewish mother and a carpenter father (again, no names given). He goes on to describe the flogging of Jesus and giving him a drink of gall and vinegar. Neither of these writers states that his birth was miraculous.

Today most scholars agree that Jesus and his apostles' existence are authenticated by both the Bible and several Jewish, Roman, and Greek historians.

Miracles of the Apostles

Some people may not know that Jesus conveyed his healing powers on to his apostles. Ten days after his ascension (Pentecost), the spirit of Christ appeared to his apostles. With tongues of fire over their heads, they spoke to multitudes in many different languages (Joel 2:28–32). The apostle Paul was hired to destroy the newly formed Christian religion. One day, the Holy Spirit of Christ appeared to him, told him to stop persecuting the Christian Church, and temporarily blinded him. This frightened him so that he immediately converted to Christianity. It was through his epistles to the nations of the eastern Mediterranean that the Christian Church experienced a mighty surge.

The apostles performed many miracles. They healed the lame, cured diseases, raised the dead, caused prison gates to open by themselves, and caused earthquakes. Paul even cured his hand from a viper bite. These miracles were witnessed by the multitudes that came to hear the apostles preach. The fact that Jesus gave his apostles such powers is further proof that Jesus was the Son of God. All four of the apostles, who wrote the gospels, agree in many instances in their writings about Jesus. How could four men have written the same things about Jesus at that same time, without the events happening?   All twelve of his apostles died martyr deaths.

Why would they have chosen a life of persecution and tortuous death unless they had truly seen the risen Christ?

One who has not read the New Testament of the Bible may ask who the apostles were. The New Testament was written between AD 60 and AD 90, twenty-five to fifty-five years after the death of Jesus. One may ask why they waited so long to write it. Speculation has it that the apostles traveled all around the Mediterranean, preaching the words of Jesus, but there was no demand for the teachings of Jesus, because Christianity did not become an important religion until years later. As the apostles founded new churches, the Christians desired to have copies of their sermons so scribes were enlisted to write their teachings into a book called the New Testament of the Bible. The New Testament is the most important part of the Bible to Christian believers, because it tells the story of Jesus's life and teachings, which are the foundation of the Christian religion. All Christians know the gospels Matthew, Mark, Luke, and John, but what did the apostles do for a living?

Matthew was a tax collector, one of the most despicable professions of that time, and yet he was welcomed by Jesus. He traveled to Palestine and all around the Mediterranean, preaching the teachings of Jesus. Matthew was a close friend of Jesus and traveled with him through most of his ministries.

Mark's home in Palestine was the meeting place of the apostles. He was a constant companion of the apostle Peter and wrote down everything Peter said about Jesus. Mark also traveled with the apostle Paul on some of his missionary journeys and became a close friend of Paul.

Luke was a physician. He too accompanied Paul on his journeys, preaching throughout the Mediterranean. He was also a companion worker of Mark. Little more is said about him.

John's mother was one of Mary's sisters, making him a first cousin of Jesus, so they probably knew each other from childhood.

He was successful in the fishing business along with the other apostles—his brother James, Peter, and Andrew. He was a disciple of John the Baptist and became an apostle of Jesus, when the baptist announced that Jesus was the son of God. He followed Jesus constantly and was the closest apostle to Jesus.

Peter was in the fishing business, as previously mentioned. He was married, and his wife followed him on all his journeys, preaching the gospels. He was a natural-born leader and, as such, became the spokesman for the twelve apostles. Jesus called him Rock and told him, "Upon this rock I will build my church." As Jesus predicted, St. Peter's Cathedral was supposedly constructed over the burial place of Peter. The remains of a body were found buried under the altar, but no means are available to determine if this is indeed the burial place of Peter. Nothing can be found about the professions of the other apostles.[15]

Jesus must have been a very charismatic leader for these men to leave their successful businesses, follow him away from their homes for years, and establish churches all over the Mediterranean for the rest of their lives.

As previously mentioned, the apostles St. Peter and James, the brother of Jesus, are mentioned by the Greek historian Eusebius, which corroborates their existence and that of the other apostles.

The Last Days of Jesus

All of the places shown on the following map have been found, which corroborates the stories in the Bible.

1. *The Last Supper.* The Last Supper took place at Coenaculum, close to the high priests' house,

---

15   Halley, Halley's Bible Handbook.

supposedly the house of the apostle Mark's mother. During the supper, Judas was exposed as the betrayer and left.

2. *The Garden of Gethsemane.* Jesus spent the evening there agonizing, because he already knew his fate. At midnight he was exposed by Judas and taken to the high priest's house. Judas, realizing what he had done, hanged himself.

3. *The High Priest's House.* Here he was accused of blasphemy for affirming that he was the son of God, was sentenced to death, and was delivered to Pontius Pilate.

4. *Pilate's Hall of Judgment.* Blasphemy was not a crime in Roman time, so Pilate sent him to Herod for his final judgment.

5. *Herod's Palace.* Here he was accused of a trumped-up charge of sedition against Rome and sent back to Pilate for sentencing. Pilate gave the Jews the choice of releasing Jesus or the criminal Barabbas, and they chose Barabbas. Pilate had no other choice but to sentence him to death by crucifixion. The wall of Herod's palace is known as the Wailing Wall, where the Jews go to pray. It was previously the wall of King Solomon's temple.

6. *Via Della Rosa* (the street of blood). Jesus was whipped, a crown of thrones placed on his head, and he was forced to carry his own cross to Mount Calvary. The street named Via Della Rosa still exists, leading from the judgment hall to Calvary.

7. *Golgotha* (Skull Hill). At Calvary Jesus was crucified on skull hill, and indeed it does have a striking resemblance to a human skull.

8. *The Tomb of Jesus.* In 1881, men digging at the foot of Skull Hill found a tomb dating back to Roman times. The tomb had been cut into the natural rock and contained a trench in front, where the stone door could be rolled. It contained no human remains. This bears a remarkable similarity to Mark 15:21–41. "In the place where Jesus was crucified there was a garden, and in the garden, a new tomb wherein was never man yet laid." The fact that all the places listed in the Scripture still exist is living testimony that Jesus was indeed crucified there.

9. *The Ascension and Pentecost.* In the forty days between his resurrection and his ascension, Jesus appeared ten times to his apostles. He appeared and disappeared through closed doors, after which he blessed them with uplifted hands and slowly rose up and disappeared in the clouds over Bethany. Ten days after the ascension, the Holy Spirit appeared to the crowd at Jerusalem with a voice of the roaring wind, and "tongues of fire" appeared above the apostles. Representatives from all the nations of the known world heard them speaking in the languages of their own countries.

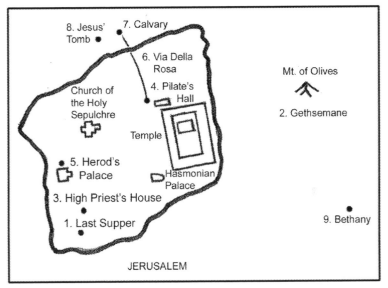

The Trial and Crusifiction of Jesus

In their book *The Bother of Jesus*, Ben Withering and Hershel Shanks investigated the recent discovery near Jerusalem in a tomb. An ancient burial box (ossuary) was found, dating to the year AD 62, which was thirty years after the death of Jesus. On the box was inscribed in Aramaic, "James, son of Joseph, brother of Jesus." Aramaic was the language spoken by Jesus. Experts agree that the box and writings are authentic. Could this be the burial tomb of the family of Jesus? Other ossuaries containing bones were found in the tomb. Perhaps DNA testing will tell us if their remains found in the tomb are related. The odds that the names would appear in that order are as low as twenty to one!

In 2008, a group of archeologists, theologians, and scientists, including Dr. Allen Callahan, Dr. Rachel Havrelock, Professor Bryan McCane, and Dr. Joan Taylor investigated the places Jesus visited on his last day. They found that all of the places that Jesus visited could be located today. The only exception was Via Della

Rosa, which exited through the west gate of Jerusalem instead of through the north gate.

The Original Bible

Obviously, we don't have any original copies of the Bible, as they have long since been destroyed. However, in 1947, copies of many books of the Bible were found written on scrolls in pots in caves just above the Dead Sea, known as the Dead Sea Scrolls. The books were written around the time of Jesus and corroborate that the copies of the Bible we now have are essentially the same as those written long ago. They even contain copies of books that were left out of the Bible during Emperor Constantine's counsel of Christian bishops at Nicaea circa AD 325. The scrolls cover a period from circa 200 BC to several decades after the crucifixion of Jesus—a remarkable find!

According to the scrolls, the people who hid these books were known as the Essenes, a Jewish sect that existed around the time of Jesus. They were related to the Maccabees Dynasty that had freed the Jews from Persian rule. However, they scorned the Maccabees because they felt their kin had become puppet followers of King Antiochus IV, so they withdrew to the wilderness around the Dead Sea at Qumran. During the Roman conquest of Israel, they hid the scrolls in caves on the cliff sides. Due to the extremely dry climate there, the scrolls remained remarkably preserved for two thousand years.

During her study of the scrolls, the noted scrolls expert Dr. Barbara Thiering discovered that the scrolls stated that a certain Essene carpenter, Joseph, was married to an Essene called Miriam (Mary in Greek) and fathered Jesus. Therefore, Jesus could have been an Essene. Thiering further records that Jesus's Sermon on the Mount had already been recorded on the scrolls—further evidence that he was an Essene. Her studies indicated that Pontius Pilate needed scapegoats to be crucified to prove that he was in control of the Jewish riot in Jerusalem. He chose Jesus. The scrolls also state that Judas Iscariot was a Jewish Zealot and a friend of Herod. Was this why Judas agreed to identify Jesus?

Michael Baigent and Richard Leigh reviewed all of the known studies done by researchers of the scrolls and noted the following amazing findings:

The scrolls mention a "Teacher of Righteousness," considered the Messiah by the Essenes, who was persecuted, tortured, and martyred. They believed that the end of the world was imminent, and only those who had faith in him would be saved. This sounds like an exact description of what Jesus preached in the New Testament. References to the Lord's Supper and the Lord's Prayer were found in the scrolls. The Essenes were awaiting a messiah, who would be of the house of David—the son of God. The scrolls continued passages that sounded remarkably like the Sermon on the Mount (The poor in spirit). The Essenes believed that the ritual of baptism would cleanse all sins, which is practiced in the Christian religion. The scrolls state that their community was governed by a council consisting of twelve members, much the same as Jesus's twelve apostles. In short, the scrolls seem to indicate that the Essenes may have been one of the first Christian sects since they practiced so many of the Christian rituals. Aside from the Bible, this further corroborates that Jesus did indeed exist.

Among the other parallels found to be the teachings of Jesus in the New Testament of the Bible are:

1. Scrolls: "Among the poor in spirit there is power."

2. New Testament: "Blessed are the poor in spirit, for theirs is the Kingdom of Heaven."

3. Scrolls: "Those who walk in perfection are commended by God."

4. New Testament: "You must therefore be perfect just as your heavenly father is perfect."

5. Scrolls: "The Council of the community shall be the tried wall, that precious cornerstone."

6. New Testament: "It was the stone rejected by the builders that became the corner stone."

7. Scrolls: "The master shall teach the saints to live accordingly to the book of Community Rule."

8. New Testament: "I must take a present of money to the saints in Jerusalem."

Two passages in the text sound remarkably like the Last Supper described in the gospels:

"When a table has been prepared the priest shall be the first to stretch out his hand to bless the bread and new wine."

"Let no man extend his hand over the bread and wine before the priest ... thereafter, the Messiah of Israel shall extend his hand over the bread."[16]

The fact that the Essene scrolls show that they believed that Mary and Joseph were the parents of Jesus; that Pontius Pilate had Jesus crucified; that their Messiah was persecuted, tortured, and martyred; that he would be of the House of David; that they believed in baptism; and that they believed in communion involving the consecration of the bread and wine corroborates many of the teachings of the New Testament.

---

16 Baigent and Leigh, The Dead Sea Scrolls Deception.

The Shroud of Turin

In 1935, a linen cloth fourteen feet long was discovered in a church at Turin, Italy. It had a negative image on the front and back of a man approximately six feet tall, indicating that he was laid on the cloth and the other half folded over him in the Jewish burial tradition. Recently when the photographic image was developed, it showed the image of a tall man with a beard and long hair, which fit the description of Jesus.

In 1968, the skeletal remains of a man that had been crucified were found in Jerusalem. A spike was still lodged in the heel bone with the piece of the wood from the cross attached to it. A nail driven into the right arm has left a groove near the wrist. Actual tests have shown that nails driven into the hands, as shown in medieval paintings, would not support the body. This offers further proof that the image shown on the shroud is correct.

In 1978, a worldwide group of scientists examined the shroud and found that the images shown on the cloth indicated that the body had been scourged (whipped) and showed wounds on the head, wrists, and side with actual blood flowing from them, indicating that he had been crucified. Scientist theorized that the image had been produced by vapors given off by perspiration caused by intense suffering, indicating a slow death by crucifixion and could not have been a forgery. Could this have been the body of Christ? Recently the shroud was tested and found to date only to the fourteenth century, but historical data showed that there was a fire in the church at that time, which could have contaminated the shroud from the smoke. Also, there have been no crucifixions since the end of the Roman era, so the fourteenth-century age could not be correct. Further testing is being performed on parts of the shroud in areas where there is no smoke damages by the Turin Shroud Center of Colorado and the Oxford University Radiocarbon Accelerator unit to determine the exact date of the shroud.

Pollen found on the shroud showed that it had been in the Holy Land. Another interesting find showed that the image on the shroud contained a three-dimensional image that could have not been produced by a painting. Furthermore, only a trace of pigment has been found on it, proving that it was not a painting forgery.

In 2009, a Vatican researcher, Barbara Fraele, using computer-enhanced images, asserted that the name Nazarene (Jesus) appeared on the shroud. This further corroborates the authenticity of the shroud. I believe that if the shroud can be dated to the time of Christ, it would help corroborate that he had been crucified.

Recent examination of the shroud indicated that it had been repaired in the area that had been tested.[17] Could this be why the shroud showed that this area dated to the fourteenth century?

MIRACLES OF THE SAINTS

The Catholic Encyclopedia and Wikipedia Free Encyclopedia on the Internet give us information on many of the saints. I have found it very difficult to accept the validity of these stories, though I have also hoped for them to be true. However, in my research, I did discover that the Catholic Church employs an impressively rigorous methodology to corroborate purported miracles. The Vatican appoints a committee of bishops and nonchurch affiliated physicians that specialize in that field to investigate each one of the miracles before they are accepted.

The requirements for sainthood set forward by the Roman

---

17   The Denver Post, May 20, 2008, November 21, 2009, April 2, 2010.

Catholic Church are that at least two healing miracles had to be performed before submittal for sainthood (beatification) and at least two miracles after submittal for sainthood (canonization). These miracles are evaluated, not only by the church, but also by eminent medical doctors, who are experts in their fields, and by the doctors treating the patients for the ailments that had been cured.

Stigmata

In the past, many saints or very religious persons bore wounds that were reportedly not inflicted by visible means. These are called the stigmata. The wounds appeared in the same places as Jesus's wounds during his crucifixion (i.e., wrists, feet, and side) and remained for their lifetimes. Some had wounds which could have been inflicted by a crown of thorns or by flogging.

The most famous stigmatic was Saint Francis of Assisi (1186–1226). His wounds were so authentic that the flesh was depressed where the nails had supposedly gone in and protruded where they exited, as if the nails were still in his body! Many of his fellow priests witnessed the wounds, as well as a number of historians of that time period.

St. Catherine of Siena (1347–1380) was the twenty-third child out of twenty-five children. Despite being born into a prosperous family, she dedicated her life to helping the ill and the poor. She died in 1380 and was interred in Rome. The people of Siena wished to have her body, but knowing that they could not get it past the Roman guards, they decided to smuggle her head out. When they got to the guards, they prayed to St. Catherine that the guards would not stop them. When the guards insisted on opening the bag containing her head, the bag was full of roses.

When they reached Siena, her head mysteriously reappeared. Because of this, St. Catherine is often pictured holding a rose.

St. Catherine de'I Ecstasies' (1522–1542) wounds began when she was twenty. They lasted for twelve years, occurring from Thursday until Friday at exactly the same time. They only ceased when she received Holy Communion. St Catherine also had wounds on all of her limbs, which imitated the scourging of Christ.

Saint Anne Catherine Emmerich (1774–1824) saw in visions of the past that the beliefs of the Roman Catholic Church were indeed true, including catechism, angels, the devil, the presence of Christ in the Eucharist, the grace of the Holy Sacraments, and the life of Christ and his mother, Mary. She saw that many saints came from the same families, some extending as far back as the Old Testament. She saw that the souls in heaven were linked to their dependents on earth, proof that we will be reunited with our loved ones. From 1802 until her death, she had wounds on her head, which replicated the crown of thorns on the head of Jesus. In 1812, she received the full stigmata, including a cross over her heart. During the last twelve years of her life, she ate no food, except the Holy Eucharist, and drank nothing but water.

Saint Gemma Galgani (1878–1903) was orphaned at the age of eighteen and worked as a housekeeper to help support her younger siblings. She was seen levitating on several occasions by other nuns in the convent. At age twenty, she developed meningitis. She prayed to St. Gabriel of Our Lady of Sorrows and fully recovered. At age twenty-one, she developed signs of the stigmata. In 1903, Gemma was diagnosed with tuberculosis and died soon after at the age of twenty-five. She is the patron saint of students and pharmacists.

Padre Pio (1887–1968) received the visible stigmata in 1918.

The wounds continued for fifty years until his death. The wounds were inspected by physicians and were found to be not self-inflicted. At Padre Pio's death, the wounds disappeared. He treated many boys during the Spanish Flu epidemic. It is documented that he performed several miraculous healings during his lifetime, even curing a blind girl. He also cured many people after his death when they prayed to him. Witnesses confirm that Padre Pio had the ability of bilocation. That is, he could appear two places at the same time. Pio even appeared to a sick boy after his death and cured the boy.

There were 321 Saints or very religious people, who reportedly received the stigmata. The most noted of these are as follows:

- Saint Francis of Assisi (1186–1226), Franciscan
- Saint Lutgarde (1182–1246), Cistercian
- Saint Margaret of Cortona (1247–1297)
- Saint Gertrude (1256–1302), Benedictine
- Saint Clare of Montefalco (1268–1308), Augustinian
- Angela of Foligno (d. 1309), Franciscan tertiary
- Saint Catherine of Siena (1347–1380), Dominican tertiary
- Saint Lidwine (1380–1433)
- Saint Francis of Rome (1384–1440)
- Saint Colette (1380–1447), Franciscan
- Saint Rita of Cassia (1386–1456), Augustinian
- Osanna of Mantua (1499–1505), Dominican tertiary

- Saint Catherine of Genoa (1447–1510), Franciscan tertiary

- Baptista Varani (1458–1524), Poor Clare

- Lucy of Narni (1476–1547), Dominican tertiary

- Catherine of Racconigi (1486–1547), Dominican

- Saint John of God (1495–1550), founder of the Order of Charity

- Saint Catherine de Ricci (1522–1589), Dominican

- Saint Mary Magdalene de Pazzi (1566–1607), Carmelite

- Marie de l'incarnation (1566–1618), Carmelite

- Mary Anne of Jesus (1557–1620), Franciscan tertiary

- Carlo of Sezze (d. 1670), Franciscan

- Margret Mary Alacoque (1647–1690), Visitandine (who had only the crown of thorns)

- Saint Veronica Giuliana (1600–1727), Capuchines

- Saint Mary Frances of the Five Wounds (1715–1791), Franciscan tertiary

- Saint Catherine de I ecstasies (d. 1542)

- Saint Gemma Galgani (d. 1903)

- Sister Catherine Emmerich (1774–1824), Augustinian

- Sister Elizabeth Canori Mora (1774–1825), Trinitarian tertiary

- Sister Anna Maria Taigi (1769–1837)

- Sister Maria Dominica Lazzari (1815–1848)

- Sister Marie de Moerl (1812–1868) and Louise Lateau (1850–1883), Franciscan tertiaries

- Padre Pio (d.1968)

Others besides the Catholic saints that received the stigmata include:

Cloretta Robinson, a Baptist from West Oakland, California, received the stigmata at age ten in 1972 during the week of Easter. She was examined by two physicians, but neither could explain the wounds that appeared on her hands, feet, side, and forehead.

In 1951, Antonia Ruffino received the stigmata after seeing a vision of the Virgin Mary. He bled from his hands and feet for over forty years.

Some of these wounds only appeared during certain days of the week. Investigations of the wounds, sometimes including twenty-four-hour surveillance, were performed by medical physicians; and they were found not to be self-inflicted and never healed until their deaths.

Levitation

Although this does not prove the existence of heaven, it does prove there is a power that some of us can tap into if we believe in it strong enough. I will discuss this power in the paranormal section of the book.

Another phenomena attributed to the saints and other spiritual people were levitation. During levitation, objects or people are lifted into the air by some unknown force. Many reputable people witnessed this phenomenon while the saint was in deep prayer. Some of the most notable were:

- Saint Maria Villani (d. 1670), who reportedly was witnessed levitating on five different occasions

- Father Paul of Moll (d. 1896), who was seen levitating for five minutes while giving Holy Communion

- Saint Gemma Galgani (d. 1903) was seen on several occasions kissing the wounds on a large crucifix on the wall while floating in the air.

- In 1615, Sister Passitea Grogi was seen levitating for at least two hours by her fellow sisters.

- Saint John of Facond (d. 1479) reportedly levitated throughout the night on several occasions.

- Saint Francis of Assisi (1181–1226) was seen suspended above the top of the tallest trees on some occasions.

- Saint Joseph of Cupertino (1603–1633) reportedly levitated for two hours.

- Saint Teresa of Avila (1526–1616) was seen levitating for nearly half an hour while in prayer.

Other saints that experienced levitation were as follows:

- Saint Francis Xavier (d. 1552)

- Sister Margret of Metola and Castello (d. 1320)

- Saint Dominic (d. 1221)

- Saint Philip Neri (d. 1595)

Being raised Catholic, I am naturally drawn to the stories of the Catholic saints. But my approach is not to prove Catholic beliefs only. There are instances of miracles, including levitation, outside the Catholic and even the Christian historical tradition. For example, the famous thirteenth century yogi of Tibet had the ability to walk, rest, and sleep during levitation. Levitation was also practiced by the Brahmins and fakirs of India, as well as the ninjas of Japan. In China, levitation has been accomplished through a "universal life force" known as the *Prana*, *Chi*, and *Ki*.

Louis Jacolliot (1884–1971) witnessed the levitation of an Indian fakir for more than twenty minutes while the fakir was uttering religious incantations. Jacolliot was told that the paranormal phenomenon was accomplished through the use of *Agasa*, the universal soul that directed all souls.

In 1906, a sixteen-year-old girl from South Africa levitated back and forth. She descended after being sprinkled with Holy Water.

In 1868, the famous psychic Daniel Douglas Home was witnessed floating out a third-story window and then back through another window by several reputable persons.

On another occasion, Home was seen floating eighteen inches off the ground. Sir William Cooke, a noted scientist of the day, passed his hand all around Home's body and could find no supporting wires. During séances, Home was known to be able to raise chairs in the air with people sitting in them. Musical instruments would float and play by themselves.

Italian medium Amedee Zuccarini was photographed levitating over twenty feet from the floor. Some scientific researchers reported that they were capable of levitating tables, and one researcher was photographed levitating a small object.

The English psychic and entertainer Doc Shiels was photographed levitating his daughter outdoors in broad daylight.

American levitator Peter Sugleris was photographed levitating outdoors in broad daylight.

The Indian rope trick, which causes a rope to remain suspended in the air outdoors in broad daylight, has never been explained. The rope remains firmly extended so that a child is able to climb it. The trick was photographed in the 1930s while being performed by Karachi and Kyder.

These instances of levitation seem to suggest the existence of a universal force that exists in an unseen dimension other than our own, which can manifest itself in our material world when called upon by spiritual believers.[18]

Indestructables

Those who wish to prove the existence of God, or at least the truth of the paranormal, can look to the seemingly unexplainable preservation of the dead. Archeological digs have revealed bodies of several saints that showed no decay and had a pleasant scent even after several centuries of burial. Many of these saints are still on display all over Europe. Since they had never been embalmed, evidence points to nothing less than a miracle. I saw the remains of Saint Francis in a glass coffin in New York City, who died in the nineteenth century, which looked perfectly preserved after over one hundred years. St. Padre Pio's body remained well preserved when it was exhumed in 2008, forty years after his death. It is now encased in a glass coffin at the shrine in San Giovanni Rotondo, Italy.

---

18   Reader's Digest Book, Unsolved Mysteries of the Past.

Prophecy

The ability to predict the future would also seem to prove the existence of the paranormal and, potentially, of the divine Many saints possessed the gift of prophecy, predicting the year and even day of their death. Such saints included Saint Frances of Rome (d. 1440), Saint Martin DePorres (d. 1637), Saint Rose of Lima (d. 1617), Saint Joseph Leonissa (d. 1612), Saint Madeleine Barat (d. 1865), and Saint Catherine Laboure (d. 1876). Saint Collette (d. 1447) predicted to the other nuns that when the big cross in the cemetery fell, their covenant would burn down. Sixty years later, the cross fell, and the covenant burned to the ground, just as she had predicted. The repetitive predictions that come to pass cannot be written off as mere coincidences.

The Consecrated Hosts

Catholics believe that the blessed bread and wine partaken in the Holy Mass represent the actual body and blood of Jesus. Several miracles have occurred with regard to the sacred host. The Catholic Encyclopedia and Wikipedia Free Encyclopedia cite the following:

In 1356, a young Catholic priest in the Cathedral of Marceta was blessing the bread and wine during mass and had doubts of it being the actual body and blood of Jesus. At the same time that he broke the consecrated host, blood (not wine) began to drip from it. The blood was authenticated by a church commission and was found to be human.

In Hasselt, Belgium, in 1317, a Catholic priest left the Host unguarded. A thief opened the container containing the Host and attempted to steal it. The Host immediately began to bleed. The frightened man fled the scene. The incident was investigated by blood testing, and the blood was found to be human.

Another incident occurred in Augsburg, Germany, circa1194. A woman secretly brought the Host home and hid it for five years. She finally returned it to the parish priest. When he finally examined it, it had turned to flesh. Although it had no odor after all of these years, it was examined in a laboratory and was found to be human flesh.

Amazing Fasts

Some of the saints and other very religious persons had the ability to fast for months and even years, partaking only of the Holy Host with no visible bodily affects. These would include Saint Catherine of Siena (d. 1380), Sister Angela of Foligno (d. 1309), Sister Catherine of Racconigi (d. 1547), Sister Elizabeth the Good (d. 1420), Saint Catherine of Genoa (d. 1547), Sister Mary De Parede (d. 1645), Saint Gemma Gaglani (d. 1903), Saint Catherine Fieschi of Genoa, Saint Ida, Saint Nicholas of Flue, Switzerland, and Saint Rose of Lima.

Eternal Fragrance

As previously mentioned, some saints emitted a pleasant fragrance when the coffins were opened long after their death. Examples were Saint Teresa of Avila (d. 1582), Saint Paul of the Cross (d. 1775), and Saint Mary Magdalen De Pazzi (d. 1607)

The Rosary

Several Jesuit missionaries survived the dropping of the atomic bomb on Hiroshima during WWII, although their home was less than a mile from ground zero. Everything around them was leveled, including the church their home was next to! Scientists have thoroughly investigated the incident and found no plausible explanation. The missionaries claim that the fact that they were praying the rosary was the miracle that saved them!

Dual Location

Another phenomena attested to by some of the saints was dual location, where someone is seen in two different places at the same time by credible witnesses. The Catholic Encyclopedia and Wikipedia Free Encyclopedia cite the following instances:

In one such incident, Saint Martin De Porres (d. 1639) had spent his entire life in Lima, Peru, yet reliable witnesses had seen him in Mexico, China, Japan, and Africa. Saint Martin himself confessed that he had also traveled to China and France by astral travel and described the visits there in incredible detail.

Saint Francis Cabrini (1850–1917) appeared to Sister Maria Pastorelli in Brazil and cured her illness, although Saint Francis was definitely in Chicago. Saint John Bosco (1815–1888) also had this ability.

Saint Catherine Del Ricci (d. 1590), who resided in Pratro, Italy, claimed that she visited Saint Philip in Rome through astral travel, even though she had never been there. Saint Philip and five other witnesses claimed that she indeed visited them by astral projection!

Saint Francis of Paola, Italy (d. 1507), in one instance, was seen both inside the church and talking to people outside at the same time. In another instance, he was seen serving Holy Communion at the altar and doing chores in the kitchen at the same time.

Saint Drogo (d. 1186) tended sheep every day, yet he was seen serving Mass at several distant churches at the same time.

Saint Vincent Pallotti (d. 1850) was seen at the deathbeds of several different people at different locations at the same time.

In 1227, Saint Anthony of Padua was reported by parishioners to have performed the Holy Mass in Limoges, France, while at the same time he was seen chanting prayers with friars in their chapel on the other end of town.

Persons other than the Catholic saints who practice dual location include:

In 1622, the native Indians in New Mexico claimed that they had been visited by a lady, who resembled a nun who had been instructing them to Christianity over fifty times. Father Alonzo de Benavides of New Mexico was perplexed, because he knew no one had been sent to instruct them. However, he had heard that a twenty-year-old nun in Spain had claimed that she had converted the natives there without leaving her convent. When Father Benavides returned to Spain, he met with Sister Mary of Jesus and asked her if she had visited the natives in New Mexico. Although she described the appearance of the Indians in great detail, she denied having visited them physically. She only suggested that an angel may have taken on her form.

Emilie Sagee was a young French teacher, who taught in a girl's school in Latvia in 1845. One day, her students reported that while she was working on the blackboard, her double appeared next to her and was mimicking her movements. In another instance, a student watching Sagee in a mirror reported that her double was helping Sagee fix the student's dress. One day, while Sagee was seen gathering flowers in the garden, she was seen by her students in the classroom at the same time. So many witnesses lend credence to these stories.

In September 1774, Bishop Alphonsus Liguori of St. Agata de Goti was observed when he fell into a deep trance at his palace near Naples. At the same time, he appeared in the chamber of the dying pope, Clement XIV, at the Vatican in Rome, assisting in the prayers and consultations. When he awoke, he described the ceremony to witnesses in detail.

Abraham Lincoln saw his double in a coffin in the White House just before his death. When he asked one of the soldiers guarding the coffin who was in the coffin, the guard replied, "It's the president, sir."

George Washington had visions that he would win the battle of Valley Forge. It was the vision that kept him fighting although it seemed like the battle was lost.

Walking On Water

In addition to the miracle of Jesus, there were other reports of this phenomenon. The Catholic Encyclopedia and Wikipedia Free Encyclopedia cite the following instances:

Saint Ammon (d. 350) was walking with Saint Athanasius when they came to a stream with no way to cross. According to the writings of Saint Athanasius, Saint Ammon immediately walked across the stream.

Saint Hayacinith (d. 1257) was told in a vision to rescue the statue of the Virgin Mary from a convent that was about to be invaded. He carried the heavy statue until he reached a large river. Many witnesses saw him walk across the river while carrying the statue with ease.

Speaking in Different Tongues

Several saints had the ability to speak to others in his own language while others understood them in their own language. The biblical precedent for this occurred during Pentecost (Acts

2:6), at which time the Holy Spirit appeared as tongues of fire over the apostles' heads. The apostles, preaching in their own language, were reportedly understood by an audience of many languages.

The Catholic Encyclopedia includes more recent stories in this vein. Saint Anthony of Padua (d. 1231) was preaching in Italian to an audience of Greeks, Latins, French, Germans, Slavs, and English. All understood him as though he was speaking their own languages.

Saint Paul of the Cross (d. 1775) was understood by people of different nationalities while preaching in Italian.

Saint Dominic (d. 1221) encountered two people who only spoke German while on a journey and was invited to dine with them. He indicated that they should pray with him. After they had prayed, they understood each other for the rest of the journey, although Saint Dominic never spoke German.

Saint Vincent Ferrer (d. 1419) was understood by as many as ten thousand people of different nationalities. This was witnessed by reputable professional people.

Padre Pio (d. 1968) heard confessions by many who spoke in their own language while he was speaking only Italian.

Other saints who had this ability were Saint Louis Bertrand (d. 1580), Saint Martin De Porres (d. 1639), Saint Philip Bernizi (d. 1285), Saint Jean Marie Baptiste Vianney (d. 1859), Saint Francis Solano (d. 1610), and Saint Bernadine of Sienna (d. 1444).

Face or Body Glows

Another phenomenon is when a person's face or entire body glows with light. Many of the saints were reported to have had this ability, including:

Saint Elizabeth of Hungary (d. 1231), Saint Clare of Assisi (d.

1253), Saint Catherine of Siena (d. 1380), Father John Ruysbroek
(d. 1381), Saint Francis of Padua (d. 1507), Saint Philip Neri (d.
1595), Saint Thomas of Villanova (d. 1555), Saint Colette (d.
1445), Saint Ignatius Loyola (d. 1556), Saint Stanislaus Kostka
(d. 1565), Saint Teresa of Avila (d. 1585), Saint Benedict Moor (d.
1589), and Saint Francis De Sales (d. 1622).

In some cases, the light was so brilliant that it dazzled the eyes
of the witnesses. This is probably why so many of the saints of the
Middle Ages are shown with halos in the paintings of that era.

Moses experienced this phenomenon when he talked to God
on Mount Sinai. His face glowed so brilliant that he had to wear a
mask to prevent blinding onlookers. The huge number of miracles
of the saints witnessed by so many reputable people cannot be
anything less than miraculous.

Healing Power of the Saints

As I have grown older, the subject of divine healing has become
more and more important to me. I have faced my own health
challenges, and I have stood with family and friends as they
faced—and sometimes succumbed to—illnesses. If there is any
area where I sincerely pray that proof of divine intervention might
be found, it would be in miraculous healing.

The Catholic Church advocates that praying to the saints can
help with every circumstance of life: Saint Anne for prolificness,
Saint Mary of Augnies for safety in childbirth, Saint Cloud for
carbuncles and boils, Saint Lambert for paralysis, Saint Apollonia
for toothaches, Saint Job for ulcers, Saint Gummarus for hernias,
and Saint Rita for critical cases. Saint Anthony helps one find lost
articles and brings prosperity in business.

St. Anthony is also known as the saint of miracles because

of his great work as an intercessor. He embraces those who are hopeless and renews their spirit. Through this intercession, the sick have been healed, the despairing have found faith, the oppressed have found freedom, the childless have conceived, the jobless have found employment, the discouraged have found hope, and, of course, lost articles have been found. Saint Anthony's great faith, human compassion, and desire to serve the Lord filled his life's journey with gifts of perfect joy!

Our Lady of the Woods helps a student pass his examinations. Saint Eligius protects the metallurgists; Saint Barbara, the miners; Saint Joseph, the carpenters; Saint Cecelia, the musicians; Saint Christopher, the travelers; and Saint Hubert, the hunters. Saint Gertrude protects against rats and mice. Saint Feuillen assures good harvests. Many Catholics have prayed to the saints and have been rewarded with their wishes.

Research on prayer as a means of curing illness suggests that it does work. In his book, Ben Sherwood cites a recent study conducted by Duke University that showed that hospital patients who were prayed for by a group of volunteers recovered much faster (beyond the laws of probability) over a group of patients with similar ailments who had not been prayed for. He further goes on to say that seven groups representing all the world's different religions prayed for ill patients. Those who were prayed for had a 25–30 percent fewer adverse effects over patients in the same group that received no prayer.[19]

Researchers at Georgia's Agnes Scott College in Atlanta, UCLA, and London's Institute of Psychobiological Research have used instruments to measure skin temperature, blood pressure, blood cell count, and encephalographs and showed that prayers had a healing effect detected on all the instruments. This effect

19   Sherwood, The Survivors Club.

can be measured even when the patient is hundreds of miles from those praying. Studies performed by the C. Maxwell Cade Research Group in England show that certain individuals have psychic healing abilities by using their mind to cure the ill.

St. Joseph is also the patron saint of realtors. My youngest son's house was on the market for a very long time. Then his realtor told him to bury a small figurine of St. Joseph in the backyard upside-down, facing the house. Within days of doing so, his house was sold. The realtor told him that it was very important that the figurine faced the house. There have been documented cases when the figurine was buried facing the neighbors house, which, in turn, sold first. Realtors claim that there is a definite correlation between burying the statue and how fast the house will sell. Several of my friends swear by it.

Saints that reputedly had the power to heal were:

Saint Antonio Claret (1807–1860), Saint John Basco (1815–88), Saint Joseph Cafasso (1811–1860), Saint Andrea Bissette (1845–1937), Saint Francis Seelos (1819–1867), Saint Kateri Tekakwitha (d. 1860), Saint Clelia Barbieri (1847–70), Saint Solanus Casey (1870–1957), Saint Francis Cabrini (1850–1917), Saint Elizabeth Seton (1774–1821), Saint Padre Pio (d. 1968), and Saint John Neumann (d. 1860).

Thousands of other miracles attributed to the above saints have been authenticated by reliable witnesses and recorded in the church documents in the parishes in which they served. Many of the cures were accomplished by prayer to these saints even after their deaths, and the cures continue to this date!

In her book *Nothing Short of a Miracle*, Patricia Treece cites the following saints, who are credited with multiple healings:

Father Solanus Casey (1870–1957), a Capuchin who served in New York, Detroit, and Indiana; Father John Newman (1812–

1860), who served in New York, Pittsburg, Baltimore, and later became bishop of Philadelphia; Mother Francis Cabrini (1855–1917), who served in New York, Central America, Denver, New Orleans, and Chicago; Brother Andre Bissette (1845–1937), who served in Montreal, Canada; Saint Elizabeth Seton, who served in New York; Saint John Bosco (1828–1888), who served all over Italy; and Father Francis Xavier Seelos (1819–1867), who served in Pittsburg and New Orleans.

In addition to performing miracles, Saint John Newman was responsible for the establishment of many schools, churches, covenants, orphanages, and other charitable institutions throughout the United States. Mother Francis Cabrini established countless day schools, hospitals, hostels for young women, and orphanages throughout the world. The retreat she founded in Denver, Colorado, in a dry mountainous area, was made possible when she struck a rock with her cane and water flowed from it. I drank from the spring a hundred years after it started flowing. Saint John Bosco established schools, workshops, training institutions, seminars, and churches throughout the world.

Among the many cures attributed to these saints through prayer were:

- blindness
- severe war wounds
- terminal cancer
- radiation poisoning
- leukemia
- deafness
- gallstones

- epileptic seizures
- meningitis,
- curvature of the spine
- dumbness
- paralysis
- hemophilia
- lip cancer
- brain tumors
- poor blood circulation
- infertility
- breast tumors
- irregular heartbeat,
- celiac disease
- chronic diarrhea
- clubfoot
- tumor of the stomach
- alcoholism
- toxemia of pregnancy
- severely burned face
- baby's underdeveloped lungs
- cardiac arrest
- lymphoma of kidneys and pelvis
- peritonitis
- fractured skull

- dislocated eyeball
- comatose
- bone cancer
- lung cancer
- drowning victim
- crippling arthritis
- psoriasis
- severe hepatitis
- cirrhosis of the liver
- retinal eye hemorrhages
- bladder cancer
- thyroid cancer
- intestinal adhesions
- kidney failure
- pneumonia
- gall bladder attacks
- paralyzed feet
- legs and arms
- diphtheria
- polio
- eczema
- degeneration of the spinal column
- asthma
- severed nerves and muscle of the arms

- crippling rheumatism
- hunchback
- cancer of the pancreas
- massive brain injury
- staph infection of the brain
- smallpox
- voice loss
- virulent influenza
- typhoid, cholera
- duodenal ulcer
- hemorrhaging blood vessel
- crushed kidneys
- lung cancer
- colon cancer
- sickle-cell anemia
- terminal liver cancer
- malignant melanoma
- bullet wound to the face
- tuberculosis
- congenital birth defects
- poisoning
- rheumatic fever[20]

Saint John Bosco is even credited with raising two people

---

20 Treece, *Nothing Short of a Miracle.*

from the dead! Some said that they experienced a wonderful wellness feeling throughout their body just before being cured.

The following is a list of some other popular saints:

- Saint Joan of Arc
- Saint Jude
- Saint Kateri Tekakwitha
- Saint Matthew
- Saint Jerome
- Saint Nicholas
- Saint Thomas Becket
- Saint Philomena
- Saint Therese of Lisieux
- Saint Josemaria de Balaguer
- Saint Lucy
- Saint Clare
- Saint Angela Merici
- Saint Leo the Great
- Saint Juan Diego
- Saint Christopher
- Saint Mary Magdalene
- Saint Anthony the Abbot
- Saint Valentine century.
- Saint Padre Pio
- Saint Roque de Santa Cruz
- Saint Anthony of Padua

- Saint Bernadette, Saint Ambrose

- Saint Rita

- Saint Augustine of Hippo

- Saint Bernard of Clairvaux

- Saint Hilary of Poitiers

- Saint James the Greater

- Saint John of Damascus

- Saint Luke

- Saint Elizabeth Ann Seton

- Saint Dominic

- Saint Monica

- Saint Rose of Lima

- Saint Teresa of Avila

- Saint Francis of Assisi

- Saint Martin of Tours

- Saint John the Baptist

- Saint John the Apostle

- Saint Thomas the Aquinas

- Saint Thomas More

- Saint Peter

A close friend of mine had a very large tumor in his abdomen. He had already scheduled the operation to remove the tumor; however, he decided to go to a faith healer anyway. The woman placed her hands on his abdomen and prayed over him. To their amazement, when he showed up for the operation, the surgeons discovered that the tumor had disappeared. My friend has attended church services nearly every day since the miracle occurred. Here again, since reputable surgeons witnessed the occurrence, this cannot be explained as other than being a miracle.

MODERN MIRACLES

Visions of the Virgin Mary

— *Fatima*

One may ask why God doesn't continue to show us miracles as proof of his existence. Many feel that he does. The following are miracles that have purportedly occurred in the twentieth

For my generation of Catholics, the story of Fatima looms large. I can remember the first time I heard the story. I became very emotional. What a wonderful sight that must have been!

Three children living near the town of Fátima in Portugal claimed to have encountered an angel in 1916 while tending their sheep. On May 13, 1917, the children witnessed a new apparition while tending sheep. They reported seeing a young woman, whose luminescent form hovered above a small oak tree. She asked the children to come to that spot on the thirteenth of every month to pray with her for the conversion of mankind to spirituality. News of the vision spread to the surrounding community, and more and more people came to watch. On July 1917, the lady showed them a frightening vision and gave them an important message that they were to keep secret until the year 1960.

The promise of a miracle on October 13, 1917, drew a throng of over fifty thousand people, despite a strong downpour of rain. The lady appeared to the children around noon. Then the sun began to spin on its axis like a pinwheel. Streamers of light came from its rim and flashed across the sky, coloring the landscape and faces of the spectators with a variety of constantly changing colors. After four minutes, the sun stopped spinning. Then it resumed its spinning and its fantastic display of varicolored light. Again it stopped and then resumed spinning for a third time, again throwing off light of different colors. Then retaining its rotary motion, the sun departed from its position and advanced toward the crowd. As the heat increased, the crowd began to pray. Just as it seemed that the sun was about to crash into the crowd, it retreated into the sky. When the people rose from their knees, they found that their clothes, which minutes before had been completely soaked, were now completely dry. The ground, too, had dried which was physical proof that the vision was indeed true.

After eight years of intensive investigation, the Catholic Church issued a letter recognizing the validity of the apparitions. The letter recording the secret message that the children received on July 13, 1917, was passed along to the Vatican. In 1967, a Vatican spokesperson disclosed that Pope Paul VI had concluded that it was not yet the proper time to reveal the contents of the message. And so, until this day, the Catholic Church has continued to guard the letter.

The famous psychic Jeane Dixon had a vision of the secret prophecy of Fatima. She saw the pope with blood running down his face (Pope John Paul II). She believed that this signaled that all Christian churches (Catholics and Protestants) would be united under one universal Christian Church (The final prophecy).[21]

There is evidence, therefore, suggesting that the lady told the children of the two World Wars and the attack on the Pope before

---

21   Dixon, A Gift of Prophecy.

they happened. Thousands have no doubt that the final "secret prophecy" will be fulfilled.

— *Lourdes*

My generation of Catholics also revered the story of Lourdes. Again, I remember the first time I heard the story. It strengthened my belief in miracles.

Lourdes is a town in France at the base of the central Pyrenees, twelve miles southwest of Tarbes. It has become a much-visited tourist center and place of pilgrimage because of the Roman Catholic religious shrine above one of the caves in the rocks, where the Blessed Virgin is said to have appeared in 1858 to a fourteen-year-old girl named Bernadette Soubirous, and from which water with healing powers is said to flow. Tens of thousands of pilgrims from all parts of the world visit the shrine annually.

The thousands of crutches left there by people who had been crippled and walked away is testimony to the miracles performed by the water. The Catholic Church and many reputable scientists have investigated the event and have recognized the authenticity of the occurrence.

In 1981, six children in Medjugorje, Yugoslavia, saw visions of the Virgin Mary and were given ten secret prophecies by her. She has appeared every year since then and given further prophecies, namely:

1. The world will receive three warnings before a great catastrophe destroys much of the earth.

2. The impending genocide in Kosovo would result in the deportation of many thousands of people. This occurred during the partition of Yugoslavia in 1991.

3. Russia would be converted. This occurred during the Reagan administration. Would the third warning prophecy the earth's destruction?

In 1961, four children in Garabanda, Spain, had visions of the Virgin Mary that continued for a number of years and predicted the following:

1. After a meteor seen around the world, Russia will be converted to the church.

2. A terrible disaster will grip the earth and two-thirds of the population will be killed.

In 1976, a child saw vision of the Virgin Mary in Finca Betania, Venezuela, which predicted the war in Asia (Iraq, 1991) and in the former Soviet Union (Georgia, 2008).

In April 1968, a vision of the Virgin Mary appeared above a church in Zeitrun, Egypt, and was seen by at least a million people. The vision was broadcast on the local TV station and photographed by hundreds of professionals. The vision lasted for three years, during which time hundreds of unexplained healings were witnessed by medical doctors. The local police searched the immediate area but found no means of photographic projection to explain the miracle.

During the Christmas season of 1996, nearly half a million people witnessed a huge multicolored vision of the Virgin Mary that appeared on the windows of a building in Clearwater, Florida. The vision lasted well into 1997, when someone attempted to remove part of the vision with an acid solution. That part disappeared for few days but then reappeared. Two noted scientists were consulted but could not explain how such an image could continue over nine panes of glass.

During 2008, a similar vision of the Virgin Mary appeared on the windows of an office building in West Springfield, Massachusetts, and was witnessed by thousands.

In September of 1995, a miracle occurred all over the globe, when millions witnessed Hindu statues drinking milk from a cup held up to their lips. TV stations and newspapers all over the world recorded the event. Scientific experts were called in but could not explain the phenomenon and declared it to be miraculous.

In March 2004 in Medford, Massachusetts, a statue of the Virgin Mary began weeping. Thousands of people witnessed the weeping.

Beginning in August 1999 in Hartford, Connecticut, crowds claimed to have seen a vision of the Virgin Mary in trees. The visions continued to appear until October 1999, when a shrine erected there was torn down.[22]

— *Paramahansa Yogananda*

The famous yogi Paramahansa Yogananda witnessed his master, Guru Sri Yukteswar, perform many miracles, including levitation, disappearing and reappearing, curing the near dead, raising people from the dead, making objects disappear and reappear (in one instance an entire palace with furnishings), caused a severed arm to be restored, and many others. In one instance, he caused a train to stop, its wheels spinning in place! This was witnessed by the startled passengers. After his death, Yogi Yukteswar appeared to Yogananda several times in a physical body so that Yogananda embraced and had conversations with him. He also appeared to other witnesses, which substantiates this.[23]

---

22 The Catholic Encyclopedia
23 Yogananda, Autobiography of a Yogi.

CHAPTER III

Angels and Demons

I have always been drawn to stories about angels and demons. At a deep personal level, it just seems true to me that such spiritual beings exist. In her book, Rene Pache devotes two entire chapters to the description of angels and Satan and quotes the Bible as her source.

Angels

The Bible declares that in the beginning, God created the heavens and the earth, and then he created the angels to serve him. Like any good organization, heaven has a hierarchy:

1. Thrones—rulers in heaven

2. Dominions—administrators in heaven

3. Principalities—administrators of nations on Earth

4. Powers—guardian angels

5. Cherubim—guards the gates of heaven with flaming swords

6. Seraphim—flaming guardians

7. Angels and archangels—messengers, guardians, warriors, servants

The Bible states that there are over one million angels. Angels have actually been seen as guardians of the weak, and in many near-death experiences they are repeatedly described as follows:

1. They emit a dazzling white light that can be seen and felt as overwhelming love.

2. They can assume human form, are larger than life, and exhibit superhuman power.

3. Contrary to popular belief, they do not have wings. This misconception was popular in the paintings of the Middle Ages, when it was felt that they needed wings to fly to heaven. The fact that they now appear without wings gives more credence to these recent sightings since the people witnessing them would have believed that they should have wings.

4. Animals can see angels while humans cannot.

5. They are superior to humans in wisdom.

6. They are humble and cover their faces in the presence of God.

7. They forbid us to worship them.

8. When God commands, they obey immediately without asking why.

9. Angels communicate through mental telepathy.

The angels are mentioned 345 times in the Old and New

Testament, so this cannot be merely people's imaginations. Their duties can be as messengers, guardians, warriors, and servants.

As *messengers*, they (1) announced the coming birth of Jesus to Mary and Joseph, (2) announced the birth of Jesus to the shepherds on Christmas Eve and sang hallelujahs, (3) rolled back the stone from Jesus's tomb and announced his resurrection to the women there, (4) presented him to Mary Magdalene, (5) participate in the government of nations, (6) comforted Jesus at the Garden of Gethsemane, (7) appeared at the ascension of Jesus and predicted his return, and (8) told Moses that he should lead his people out of Egypt and gave him the Ten Commandments.

As *guardians*, they (1) protected the child Jesus when he traveled to Egypt, (2) saved Daniel from the lion's den and his friends from the fiery furnace, (3) watched over the Israelites on their journeys to and from Egypt, and (4) aided Jesus after his temptation by Satan in the desert.

As *warriors*, (1) they protected Israel and fought the demons that seek to harm that nation. (2) They destroyed a whole Assyrian army in 600 BC, when it attacked Israel. (3) The angel Gabriel and his angels fought a battle with Satan and his fallen angels in heaven and cast them down to Earth.[24]

In their book, Craig Lundahl and Harold Widdison site well-documented accounts of the angels as protectors:

- In the eighteenth century, a large army of angels with drawn swords on white horses confronted a warring tribe of natives in Brazil. The natives were intent on attacking a recently converted Christian village. When they saw the huge army, they fled in fear.

24 Pache, The Future Life.

- A well-documented account concerns a World War I battle in Mons, France. The allied soldiers had suffered a terrible defeat, when the Germans' horses suddenly turned and fled. Allied troops said they had seen angels on the battlefield. When asked why they fled, the Germans replied that they had seen thousands of allied soldiers guarding the position. The allies only had two regiments.

- Recently they protected two helpless women from encounters with murderers in two separate instances. The women later identified the criminals in a police lineup. The criminals were asked why they did not kill the women, and they replied that they had seen two of the largest most powerful men that they had ever seen with the women and knew that they would have been destroyed immediately if they had tried to harm the women. The women never saw their protectors. The occurrences were documented by two police departments.[25]

As *servants*, they (1) carry on the daily operations in heaven, (2) serve as escorts for those who have died so that they may find the tunnel of light leading to heaven, (3) protect departed souls from the demons that are trying to stop them when they are searching for the light to the entrance of heaven, and (4) protect the gates of heaven from demons trying to enter.

In the book of Daniel, God showed the prophet the unseen world of good and evil entities of superior intelligence, which are controlling all the nations on Earth. Some of them were protecting God's people. The others were striving to destroy the

---

25   Lundal and Widdison, The Eternal Journey.

church and causing wars and natural disasters. God was showing Daniel the secret agencies in action. Satan and his demons of the unseen world are the chief enemies of the church.

SATAN AND HIS DEMONS

Satan

The character of Satan as being a red entity with horns, pointed ears, and a barbed tail came from an artist of the Middle Ages, associating him with the fiery red flames of hell. Actually, Satan can take on many forms—i.e., human (male or female), a serpent, a lion, a lamb, an angel of light, a seven-headed dragon with ten horns, a wolf, and a leopard.

Satan was a Principality and a Power, two of the most powerful positions in heaven. When God created Adam, he told all of his angels to bow down before Adam. Satan refused because he felt that he was superior to a mere mortal. He then conspired with other angels in a revolt against God so that he could become God's equal. When God found out that Satan was conspiring against him, he became very angry. He directed his warrior archangel, Michael, and his army of angels to engage Satan in battle. Satan and his fallen angels were defeated, and God directed that they be cast out of heaven to earth to await the final judgment. Satan then became recognized as the devil and his fallen angels as demons. God allows him and his demons to roam the earth, testing humankind to see if we are worthy of entering the kingdom of heaven.

Satan has many names in the Bible:

- the tempter
- the devil

- the dragon
- the serpent
- the accuser
- the deceiver
- the liar
- the murderer
- the day star (before his fall)
- the prince of the world
- the destroyer of nations
- the cherub
- the lord of evil spirits
- the angel of the abyss (hell)
- the power of the air
- the prince of demons
- the god of this world
- the thief
- the wolf
- the lion.

Satan is spoken of in the Bible as many times as the angels (345 times). This cannot be only peoples' imagination. He is so powerful that even Michael the archangel refrains from judging him harshly. Jesus called him the Prince of the World because Satan controls all of the nations of the world. He still has access to God to make accusations against us.

In the book of Job, Satan (humanity's accuser) tells God that the only reason that Job, a very prominent rich man, is faithful is because Job had received so many gifts. God denied that was true and told Satan that he could test Job. First, Job's vast herds of camel and oxen were stolen. Then seven thousand of his sheep were killed by lightning. All his children were killed by a cyclone, and finally, Job was smitten with leprosy.

Job's friends suspected that he was being punished for some kind of wickedness that he was hiding and urged him to repent for his sins. Not being a sinner, Job reaffirms his faith in God. Finally, believing that Job has withstood all his trials successfully, God rewarded him and granted him a long life.

The Tribulation will be the last desperate outburst of the devil, after which he will be chained for one thousand years in the abyss (hell). He will then be released to tempt mankind again, after which he will be cast into the lake of fire and brimstone (hell) and be tormented for eternity.

Satan's first triumph over God was convincing Adam and Eve to eat the forbidden fruits, deposing God's creations forever from the Garden of Eden. He tempted Jesus three times while he was in the desert, promising him power over the whole world. He especially tempts God's servants and spiritual leaders, because they are dangerous to him—i.e., popes, priests, and other Christian ministers.

During the Tribulation, Satan will speak as if he were preaching the teaching of God (as a false Messiah, a deceiver). The Antichrist will be the servant of the devil and will have all of his powers. He will persuade everyone that he is Christ and persuade us to worship him by performing miracles.

Satan exaggerates that our sins are unpardonable and that we should worship him. He has caused firestorms from the skies, hurricanes, and floods. Satan's second triumph was that he caused the Pharisees and Pontius Pilate to crucify Jesus. Christ destroyed Satan's power over us with his death. All the suicides and wars are his doing. He will cause atomic destruction during the Tribulation.

Demons

The demons are the fallen angels that followed Satan during his unsuccessful attempt to take over heaven. Satan and his demons were cast out of heaven by the archangel Michael and his warrior angels. The Pharisees, with the encouragement of Satan, had Jesus crucified, because they thought that he would rally his people against Rome, and then the Romans would relieve the Pharisees of their positions.

Examples of demonic possession are pedophiles, serial killers, rapists, and other evil people. The demons are attacking the Church. A multitude of them opposed Christ's teachings in Palestine. During the Tribulation, Satan and his demons will fight one last time against Michael and his angels at Armageddon, near Jerusalem (Rev. 18:2). Babylon (Iraq) will become a habitation of demons (terrorists). This is now happening as predicted!

Demons, deprived of a body, take possession of humans to satisfy their passions. Demons took possession of the people of Sodom and Gomorrah, so God destroyed the cities. Legions of demons were cast out of the demoniac of Gadara by Jesus and were placed into swine. There, demoniacs described by Matthew were so powerful that not even chains could hold one of them. Contact (Ouija boards and séances) with the spirits has resulted in possession by them, resulting in many disorders. Possession by demons can cause illnesses and infirmities (e.g., boils, dumbness, blindness). Jesus drove seven demons out of Mary Magdalene. The devil will possess the Antichrist and will give him great powers so that he will deceive us into believing that he is the true Christ by performing miracles.[26]

Personal Reflections

As I reflect on these materials about angels and demons, I have a very personal reaction. I feel a strong sense of hope in the existence of angels and a dread that demons also exist. I fear you cannot have one without the other.

---

26 Pache, The Future Life.

CHAPTER IV

Psychic Phenomena

Up until this point, I have presented historical events and materials mostly from the Bible and official church sources. Now I turn to a very different body of evidence and one around which I have many more personal experiences, namely, psychic phenomena, including precognition or prophecies, near-death experiences, reincarnation, exorcism, astral travel, psychokinesis, mental telepathy, and remote viewing.

Precognition—Personal Experiences

Precognition or prophecies can be described as the ability to predict the future. I have had several instances of precognition. One involved the death of my grandfather, who lived on the East Coast of the United States. Before his death, I dreamed that I was in a shallow grave in his front yard, pulling dirt onto myself. Later my mother told me that she had asked him if she should call and tell me to come because he was dying. He replied, "Don't call him. I will inform him." I then realized that this was his way of telling me he was dying.

Another incident occurred when I was taking flying lessons. The night before I was supposed to take the airplane out for the first time. I dreamed that the wings had fallen off the airplane. The next day, I only opened two of the four hangar doors, and as I pulled the airplane out, I put two big dents in the wings. A third instance involved a dream in which I dreamt that a certain person who I worked with was involved in an automobile accident. The next day when I inquired why that person had not showed up for work, I was told that he had been in as serious auto accident.

In another incident, I dreamed that I was sitting beside someone with a thin mustache in a hearse. Several days later, a friend of mine died. When I went to the funeral, I saw the collage of his early pictures and was amazed. In several of the pictures, my friend had a thin mustache. I never knew that my friend ever had a mustache. Could this be more than a mere coincidence? Two years ago, I had a strong premonition that something was going to happen to my wife's sister. Although we were well into winter in Denver, I convinced my wife that she should visit her sister. The day that she left, they had to deice the airplane, and there was a four-hour delay because of a snowstorm. A month later, her sister had to have heart surgery, but she did recover.

Recently I dreamed that I witnessed the door being torn off of a vehicle. A few days later, I met a friend that I had not seen for a while. When I asked where she had been, she replied that she had been involved in an automobile accident and had lost her driver's license because her eyesight had deteriorated. Later we found out that she had taken the door of another vehicle off with her car!

In another recent dream, I saw a car window being shattered. The next day, our daughter-in-law called and told us that one of the windows of our grandson's car had been shattered. The sudden occurrence as predicted had to be more than mere coincidence!

While watching a local TV station, I sensed that death was close to the TV announcer. Soon after, his son was killed on a roller-coaster ride.

All of these experiences cannot be mere coincidences and seems to indicate we have a sixth sense that we once had to warn us of danger and have lost after we become civilized.

PROPHECIES OF THE BIBLE

Armageddon

Like many people, I wonder how human life will end. Are we moving to some monumental culmination of history? Will I live to see it? On the one hand, it is terrible to imagine. On the other hand, it would be the irrefutable proof that many of us have long awaited.

In Revelation 6:12–17, 16:12–21, and 8:7–13, the Bible describes the end of the world in four stages: Tribulation, the second coming of Christ, Judgment Day, and world destruction. During the Tribulation (2012), the Antichrist emerges as the leader of his army (all the demon armies of the past would be resurrected). At first, the Antichrist befriends Israel. But after three and a half years, he begins a horrible persecution of the Jews (Dan. 9:24–27; Matt. 24:15–22). Because of this, Israel begins to return to God. At the height of his persecution of God's people, the Antichrist's own worldwide power base begins to crumble. The battle of Armageddon begins when the king of the north (Russian?) and the king of the south (Arabs?) converge in Israel to attack the Antichrist and his troops. After these armies are defeated, the king of the east (China?) invades Israel, resulting in the final campaign of Armageddon (Rev. 16:16).

Revelation 9:3, 9:7 describes the battle. "Shapes of locustlike war horses with scorpion like tails ... faces like men's faces ... teeth like lion's teeth, breast plates as of iron, and wings that sounded like horses and chariots to war." Sounds like modern-day attack helicopters with their long skinny tails, their blades chopping the air, and heavily armored men at the controls. Some even have sharks' teeth painted on them, like the old World War II flying tigers.

"Smoke from the abyss" (Rev 9:2, 3) could refer to the smoke from the exploding rockets and bombs (Rev. 9:12–21). "Horrible looking monsters of complex appearance … belching fire, smoke and brimstone"—this could refer to modern-day tanks, with their turning tracks and shooting canons. What an accurate prediction of what is to come made two thousand years ago!

During the seventh year of the war (2019), Christ will appear on a cloud from heaven. He will assemble his warrior angels under Michael the archangel and engage the devil and his demon armies in the final battle at Medigo (Armageddon), near Jerusalem. The devil and his armies will be defeated, and they will be chained and thrown into the lake of fire (hell), where they will remain for one thousand years (Rev. 19:19–21).

The final judgment would then begin. The faithful dead will arise and ascend into heaven. The unfaithful dead will arise and those found unworthy of heaven will be judged and tortured for eternity. (This seems unbelievable for a forgiving God. However, he has let the devil persecute the Jews for all of history through the Assyrian, Babylonians, and Roman rule; the Spanish Inquisition; and the Nazi holocaust for not following his commandments.) The living will be judged, and the unfaithful will suffer the same consequence as the unfaithful dead. The faithful will never die, and their lifespan will be greatly extended. One hundred years of age will be a young man.

After Judgment Day, there will then be peace on Earth for one thousand years (3019), after which the earth will be destroyed.

In the Bible's book of Revelation, the apostle John gives a vivid description of the end of the world:

- There was a great earthquake, and the sun became black as sack cloth, and the moon became as blood. (Rev. 6:12)

- And the stars of the heaven fell upon the earth. (Rev. 6:13)

- And the heavens departed ... and every mountain and island was moved out of their places. (Rev. 6:14)

- There will be hail and fire mingled with blood, which will burn up one-third of all the trees and grass. A great mountain burning with fire will be cast into the sea, causing one-third of the sea to turn to blood, killing a third of its creatures. (Rev. 8:8–12)

- Then a great burning star will fall upon a third of the rivers and springs, making the waters bitter and causing many to die. A third of the sun, moon, and stars will be darkened ... for a third part of the day. (Rev. 8:7–13)

- Horribly painful sores will break out on people who have submitted to the beast (Antichrist). (Rev. 16:2)

- The sea will turn to blood and all aquatic life will die. (Rev. 16:3)

- The water in springs and rivers will turn to blood. (Rev. 16:4)

- The sun is allowed to burn the people. (Rev. 16:8)

- Darkness will cover the earth. (Rev. 16:10)

- The great Euphrates River will dry up. (Rev. 16:12)

- A devastating earthquake, accompanied by hail, alters the surface of the earth. (Rev. 16:17–21)

In his book, Paul A. LaViolette, PhD, gives a scientific explanation to all of these prophecies. He believes that huge gravitational waves coming from exploding stars could cause earthquakes and tidal waves. He cites the December 26, 2004, earthquake that struck Sumatra as an example. On December 27, gamma ray telescopes orbiting the earth received the largest gamma ray burst from a star ever recorded. Explosions of this magnitude are likely to produce gravity shock waves, which would have preceded the gamma ray burst since they are initially faster than the speed of light. Gravity wave occurrences have been studied by several physicists since the 1960s and have discovered that they can become more intense at times.

The star that exploded on December 26, 2004, in Sagittarius A is located at the center of our Milky Way Galaxy, approximately twenty-five thousand light-years away, where there are millions of red giant stars, any of which could explode any minute. In 1987, a star known as Sanduleak -69° 202a was seen exploding and became hundreds of times brighter. Also in 1987, Supernova 1987A exploded, glowing hundreds of times brighter than what it looked like in 1984. The first time a star in Sagittarius A exploded was on October 26, 2000. It brightened to forty-five times its original size in a few minutes and then returned to its original brightness within a period of three hours. Sagittarius A is twenty-five thousand light-years away. There are many stars as close as eleven light-years from Earth. Should a star much closer to the earth explode, the gravitational wave produced could cause the earth to tilt on its axis far enough to displace the oceans, leaving the tops of high mountains as the only habitable dry land. This was dramatically portrayed in the movie *2012*. Astronomers are keeping a close eye on all of the stars close to Earth that could possibly explode.

LaViolette goes on to say that there are huge clouds of cosmic dust that our solar system passes through on our journey around the center of our galaxy, toward which we are now headed. These could be responsible for the darkening of the sun and reddening of the moon, as mentioned in Revelation 8:12. He further states that a cosmic dust invasion could be responsible for the drying up of the rivers and lakes, because the dust could cause the earth to heat up. Acidic rain, caused by the dust, could cause painful sores. Solar flares have been recorded in the past, which have traveled well beyond the distance to the earth but, luckily, in another direction. This could cause the scorching of the earth.

The Next Ice Age

As previously mentioned, Supernovas occur when huge stars explode, sending debris to immense distances across the universe. La Violette describes one such incident that occurred approximately one million years ago between the constellations Lupus and Centaurs that was only 425 light years away from the earth. The remnant named the North Polar Spur covers most of the southern sky. Scientists can measure that the earth is now being engulfed in this debris, which has dramatically affected the earth's climate, causing the ice ages to become much more severe. This debris could also contain meteors and comets, which could impact the earth and cause massive destruction.

Should the dust the earth is now passing through become denser, it could block out sufficient sunlight and cause the earth to cool down and send us into another ice age. The ice core samples taken in the Greenland ice cap indicate that the earth has gone through seven ice ages in the last 20 billion years. The last ice age ended approximately twelve thousand years ago. Graphs produced in the Porter Quaternary Research Report measuring the oxygen isotope climate levels at the equator indicate that the major warm interglacial periods for the last four hundred thousand years averaged approximately sixteen thousand years. The graph shows that we are on the steep downward side of the peak and could be plunged into another ice age within one thousand years!

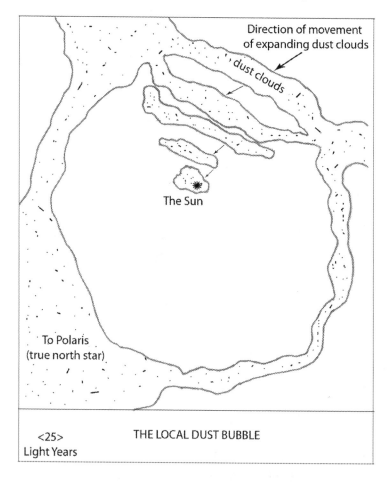

The Local Bubble

The included figure shows the giant bubble of dust and gas that surrounds our solar system (local bubble). Scientists theorize that the bubbles are formed by the explosion of a supernova that compresses the clouds of dust into bubble shapes. In other words, this bubble assumes a spherical shape around our solar system. The rapidly expanding bubble of dust running across the top right is now bearing down on the local bubble, pushing streamers of gas and dust ahead of it, and is now sweeping past our sun. As previously mentioned, should the dust clouds get too dense, they could cause the next ice age by blotting out too much of the sun's rays.

The Center of Our Galaxy

The center of our galaxy contains an intense radio emission source, Sagittarius A. Scientists are not sure what Sagittarius A actually is. It could be a black hole as massive as a million stars. The galaxy's center is surrounded by a ring of moving gas and dust clouds. A tiny point of light appears at the center as brilliant as the quasar stars (flashing stars) that appear in the other galaxies. Professor Violette theorizes that a shock wave caused by an exploding star in Sagittarius A supposedly caused the tidal wave that was so destructive in Sumatra in 2004.

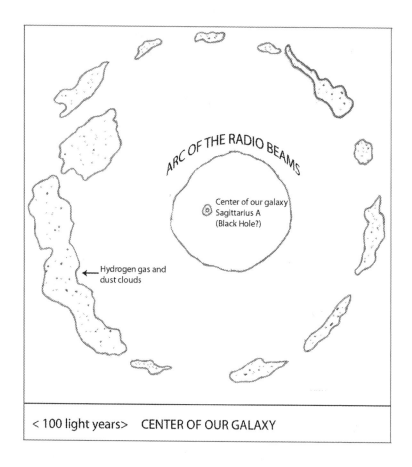

< 100 light years>　CENTER OF OUR GALAXY

The center of our galaxy can be found on a clear evening, low in the southern horizon, and midway between the constellations Sagittarius, the half man, half horse, and Scorpius, the scorpion. Ancient Greek legend has it that Sagittarius is aiming his arrows at the heart of Scorpius, which at that time in history would have passed directly through the galactic center in its flight. As shown on the below illustration, Sagittarius resembles a teapot with a handle, lid, and spout. The ancients believed it was an archer and that the spout was the arrow aimed at Scorpius. Scorpius does resemble a scorpion with a stinger tail and a head with arms that look like claws. The end of the tail points directly to the galactic center. Scientists believe that the galactic core was exploding at that time and would have appeared much brighter to the ancients, and that is why they chose these two constellations to locate it.[27]

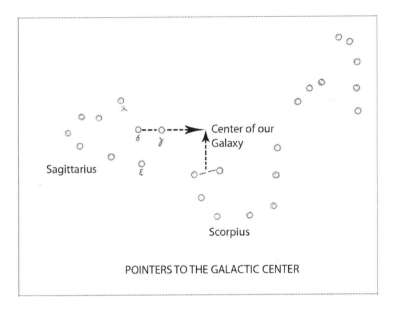

POINTERS TO THE GALACTIC CENTER

The End of the Universe

Astronomers theorize that the universe was created 12 billion years ago, after a tremendous explosion at its center, which sent debris out in all directions (the big bang theory). As it expanded, it began to cool down, and hydrogen and helium were produced. Gravity caused some of the hydrogen gas to compress under tremendous pressure, forming stars. The pressure was so intense that the hydrogen ignited and created nuclear reactions. As some of the stars consumed most of their hydrogen, they collapsed upon themselves due to low gravity, creating the heavier elements we

27   La Violette, Earth under Fire.

know today (e.g., iron, lead, gold, etc.) Some of these elements coalesced to form asteroids, some of which were attracted to each other and eventually formed the planets. A ring of asteroids circles the sun between Mars and Jupiter, which never formed into a planet.

But how will the universe end? Right now, astronomers can measure that all the stars and galaxies are moving away from each other at around the speed of light. The big question is, will it eventually slow down and start to implode, causing another big bang? If there is enough mass in the universe, gravity will cause this expansion to slow down and eventually reverse its directions. Scientists believe that there is a lot more mass in the universe than is visible to the naked eye; otherwise, gravity would not be sufficient to keep the galaxies from flying apart since the stars are orbiting their galaxies much too fast to keep them together (dark matter).

Scientists now believe that the dark matter may be located in the black holes at the center of the galaxies or invisible dead stars, which do not shine, or planets, which reflect no light because they have no stars to shine on them. However, we should not be concerned, because this reversal, if it occurs, will take several billion more years.[28]

After the Sumatra earthquake of 2004, scientists measured the inclination of the earth and found that it had changed a fraction of a degree. The March 2010 earthquake in Chile caused the time of the rotation of the earth to slow down a fraction of a second. Ice cores taken deep within the glaciers in Greenland indicate that the Arctic was a much warmer place twenty thousand years ago, which could have been caused by a major shift in the inclination of the earth. Magnetic rocks found dating back to

28 Levy, Skywatching.

that time corroborate that the magnetic poles had indeed shifted. Such a shift could have been caused by several major earthquakes occurring simultaneously, resulting in tsunamis and volcanoes erupting and falling into the sea.

The March 2011 earthquake in Japan caused a thirty foot tsunami that leveled one of Japans major cities.

The earth's crust averages only twenty miles in thickness and is divided into several tectonic plates—weak points in the crust. The thickness may be only five miles beneath the oceans. These plates are constantly in motion. The force of gravity due to the weights of the plates and the centrifugal force caused by the earth's rotation produce tremendous stress on the plates, which causes them to crack at the weak points, resulting in seismic energy waves. The waves that travel laterally from their point of origin are harmless, but those that travel perpendicular from their origin can cause tremendous damage.

Most of the serious earthquakes are confined to two belts. One follows the coastline of Chile up to the Western Coast of the United States, Canada, Alaska, and the Aleutian Islands and then goes south through Japan, the Philippine Islands, and Indonesia; this is called the Ring of Fire, because so many volcanic eruptions occur along this fault. The other belt runs eastward from Spain through the Mediterranean, Turkey, the Caucasus Mountains, and the Himalayas to the Malay Peninsula and Indonesia, where it intersects with the Pacific Belt.[29]

In Revelation 6:12 and 16:17–21, John states that "a devastating earthquake will alter the surface of the earth." The many devastating earthquakes we are now witnessing may indicate that the earth is in grave unbalance. Revelation 8:7–8 states, "A great burning star will fall upon a third of the rivers and springs making the

29 The World Book Atlas

waters bitter and causing many to die." A huge asteroid striking the earth could destroy a large city, and the fallout debris would circle the earth for several years, shading the sun and sending the earth into another ice age. Hundreds of large meteors striking the earth at the same time could cause massive fires. Two huge asteroids have passed the earth as close as the moon in the last two years. Nearly eight hundred huge asteroids have been discovered that pass within the earth's orbit, some measuring more than a half mile wide, according to NASA's Near-Earth Object Program. Over six thousand other asteroids have been discovered, which come within the earth's orbit. Should one of these asteroids strike the earth, it could possibly cause the end of civilization. In 1908, a large asteroid exploded in the earth's atmosphere over Siberia, which leveled nearly eight hundred square miles of trees. Scientists are studying the possible ways of diverting any huge asteroid from hitting earth, such as pushing them with rockets. Making it explode with a nuclear device would cause it to fall in smaller pieces, which would still be a danger. In 1993, one came within ninety thousand miles of the earth, well within the orbit of the moon. On September 5, 2010, two asteroids did so, one as large as sixty-five feet in diameter—large enough to destroy a city. We were given little advance notice. In 2026, an asteroid the size of three football fields (Apophis) will pass within two hundred miles of the earth. In 2038, it will enter the earth's atmosphere. If it hits the surface, it could destroy a state as large as Texas. If it hits in the ocean, it will cause a tsunami, which would travel hundreds of miles inland.

The April 2010 volcanic eruption, which occurred under a glacier in southern Iceland, threw up such a massive quantity of ash containing fine glass that thousands of flights were cancelled and millions of travelers were stranded on both sides of the Atlantic.

This volcanic ash has clogged jet engines in the past, causing them to shut down. Iceland is situated on the Atlantic Ridge, which traverses the middle of the Atlantic Ocean and produces several under-ocean volcanoes. Iceland contains as many as one hundred volcanoes, twenty-five of which have been active in the past. Some of these volcanoes have been ten times more powerful than the 2010 one that erupted. Mount Hekla is known to have erupted on nineteen occasions. In 1783, the volcano Laki erupted, spewing lava, ash, and gas, which caused glaciers to melt, causing massive floods. Hundreds of acres of farmland were covered with ash, making them useless, and 80 percent of the island's livestock were destroyed. Over nine thousand people were killed. The ash cloud turned red because of the acidic gas from the eruption. This could explain the prophecies in Revelation 6, 8, and 16, where it states that "the moon will become as blood," "there will be hail and fire mingled with blood," "one-third of the sea will turn to blood," and "the water in springs and rivers will be turned to blood." In Revelation 6:14, John predicts, "Every mountain and island was moved out of their places." In 1883, the volcanic island of Krakatau erupted, leveling most of the island. The tsunami caused by the underground earthquake produced a fifty-foot-high wave that traveled as far as eight thousand miles. Thousands of people were killed and properties along the coast of Java and Sumatra were leveled. The volcano erupted again in 1927.[30]

The Book of Daniel

Daniel was a young man when the Babylonians sacked Jerusalem. Because they thought he would be useful, they took him back to Babylon. He became one of King Nebuchadnezzar's favorite

---

30 Funk & Wagnalls Encyclopedia

advisors because he had the gift of prophecy and correctly interpreted the king's dreams. The king trusted Daniel, so he put him in charge of all the wise men in Babylonia. The men were so infuriated that they devised a scheme to get rid of Daniel. They informed the king that the Jews would not worship the Babylonia gods. Three of Daniel's friends were threatened to be cast into a fiery furnace if they did not bow down to the Babylonia gods. Because they did not comply, they were thrown into the furnace and the door was sealed. When the king opened the door and called to them, he was astonished when they replied. He told them to come out, and when they did, they were unharmed and did not even smell of smoke. The king believed that it was their god that had saved them and put to death their accusers. The wise men that tried to trick Daniel advised the king to issue a decree disallowing Jews to pray to their god for thirty days. Daniel continued to pray anyway. The king was again infuriated with Daniel and had him thrown into a den full of lions. The king was sorry for what he had done and called to Daniel. When he replied, the king was amazed and told him to come out. He finally believed that indeed Daniel's God was a powerful God. A cameo was found in Babylon bearing the likeness of King Nebuchadnezzar.

In his final chapters, Daniel gives us a prophecy of the end of the world. "There shall be trouble such as never was, followed by resurrection of the dead (Rapture) (Daniel 12). Torture, suffering, and death of whole populations by demon dictators (such as Hitler, Stalin, Milosevic, Saddam Hussein, Osama bin Laden, the Antichrist, etc.) unparallel in all the previous history. "Many shall run to and fro, and knowledge shall be increased" (Daniel 12). The computer, the Internet, and the rise from the horse and buggy to the space age in one century has caused the dissemination of knowledge faster than any other period in history.

Jesus said, "On the earth distress of nations in perplexity for the roaring of the sea, men fainting for fear, and expectation of the things that are coming to the world" (Luke 21:25–26).

PROPHETS OF FUTURE EVENTS

Several famous prophets include Nostradamus, Jules Verne, Tennyson, Edgar Cayce, and Jean Dixon. Many of their predictions that have been documented have come to pass with amazing accuracy.

Nostradamus (1503–1566)

Nostradamus, born Michele De Nostradamus, was a sixteenth-century physician, astrologer, and prophet, who lived in southern France. Nostradamus received his visions of the future, not in a crystal ball but in a vessel filled with water. He recorded them in ten books, which he called the "Centuries" and contains 1,600 prophecies. Many of these prophecies proved true in his lifetime, and many others have been confirmed throughout the centuries. The following describes some of the more famous prophecies described in the "Centuries."

In 1700, grave robbers opened his tomb and found a medallion with the number MDCC (1700) engraved on it, as if to predict when it would be opened! One of them, thinking that he would inherit Nostradamus's powers, drank from his skull. He had not heard the prediction that "whoever disturbed this grave would soon die." He was soon struck dead by a stray bullet from a nearby battle.

One of his most famous predictions was the announcement that Felice Peretti would be elected pope soon after they met. Nineteen years after Nostradamus's death, Peretti was elected pope (Pope Sixtus V).

Another famous prediction was the death of King Henry II. "The old lion would be killed by a young lion on a warlike field [joist] by one of two piercings." Six years later, he was killed in a jousting tournament by Montgomery, captain of the Scottish guards, when his lance broke in two pieces and one penetrated the slit of his visor.

On July 1, 1566, Nostradamus told his pupil Chavign that he would not be there at sunrise and was given the last rites. He was found dead at this workbench the next morning.

Other predictions attributed to Nostradamus include:

- The Great Fire of London (1666)
- The French Revolution (1789–1792)
- The Napoleonic Wars (1803–1815)
- The American Revolutionary War (1775-1783)
- The American Civil War (1861-1865)
- The assassination of Abraham Lincoln (1865)
- The rise of Hitler (1939–1945)
- The civil war in Spain (1936-1939)
- Abdication of Edward VIII (1972)
- The atomic bomb (1945)
- Manned rockets to the moon (1969)
- Rise of the Ayatollah Khomeini (1978)
- The Kennedy assassinations (1963 and 1968)

— *Future Predictions of Nostradamus:*

A country on the east coast of the Mediterranean (Israel?) will be attacked with a nuclear bomb by a country in the Middle

East (Iran?). They (Israel?) will retaliate with a nuclear bomb. The Middle Eastern country will then unleash nuclear bombs on Italy and France. The Western countries and Europe (US and England?) will intervene to protect the oil supply.

The appearance of a new comet will signal the start of several natural disasters. Earthquakes and volcanic eruptions will cause famine and drought. This will cause worldwide rioting. Masses of people will be forced to migrate to escape the famine, which will create a civil upheaval. A great nation (US or England?) will be bankrupted by the natural disasters, but three other nations will send help.

The Antichrist will appear in the year 2012 and will first use his power to restore peace to the world. He will be a young dark man from the Middle East. The Antichrist will get an antipope elected (Peter the Roman).

The Antichrist will send his troops to Central Europe and the Near East in the disguise of helping the victims but instead will take over these countries.

A comet will announce the death of a leader from the Middle East. After his death, widespread crop failures will cause a riot that will continue for one and a half years.

Near the coast of South America, a US naval vessel will accidently ram a Soviet submarine. The event will cause tension between the two nations.

The Electoral College will be evenly split during the election of the next US president. The ensuing tension will be settled by a new election.

The earth will enter into an ice age, causing the crop-producing regions to freeze. Famine will cause millions to flee to warmer climates. Poor decisions made by the United States and the United Kingdom will escalate the situation.

The Antichrist, with the assistance of the Soviet Union and the Arabs, will start World War III, beginning with the destruction of New York City. During the second coming of Christ, in the second millennium, Christ will destroy the Antichrist and his army and restore peace. There will then be two thousand years of peace; the world will end in 3797.[31]

Most of his predictions were made centuries before the events came to pass.

Leonardo daVinci (1452-1519)

Although Leonardo was not a psychic, he was a superb visionary. He was born in the town of Vinci in Italy in 1452 to a housemaid and a wealthy Florentine man. He was raised by his father after he convinced his mother that he would be better off with him. In addition to his painting, Leonardo was an excellent scientist, biologist, architect, engineer, mathematician, and inventor. When he was fifteen, his father sent him to Florence, the Renaissance capital of the world, where he studied under the master painter Verrocchio. Leonardo soon painted a number of masterpieces and was well-known in the art circle. His most famous painting was *The Last Supper*. Amazingly, the church where he painted it was bombed during the Second World War, and only the wall surviving had the painting on it.

In 1482, he became the military advisor to the Duke of Milan and designed military weapons that were very futuristic, including a tank, a multibarrel cannon, a helicopter, a parachute, a flying machine, a submarine, and an automobile. Several full-scale models of his designs were built recently, and many were workable.

---

31   Lean, Nostradamus and His Prophecies.

In 1506, he completed his second most famous painting, *Mona Lisa*. At the age of sixty-five, he became an architect, painter, and an engineer for the king of France, Francis I. Leonardo died in 1519 at the age of sixty-eight. He recorded all of his observations and inventions in notebooks, which were not published until 1881. Had they been published sooner, they would have advanced science and engineering hundreds of years ahead of the times.

The Brahan Seer (born 1600)

The most famous of all of Scotland's seers, Kenneth Mackenzie, better known as the Brahan Seer, was born in the sixteenth century in the highlands of Scotland. Mackenzie's mother claimed that she received mystical powers from a ghost, who had given her a magical stone which she gave to him. Mackenzie successfully predicted nuclear fallout, the advent of railways, and the discovery of North Sea oil. He predicted the start of a worldwide conflict if a fifth bridge was built across the River Ness. In August of 1939, a fifth bridge was constructed across the river. On September 1, Hitler invaded Poland and World War II started.

His most famous prediction was associated with the Brahan Castle, and hence, he became known as the Brahan Seer. Because of his fame, he was hired by the wife of the Earl of Seaforth, who lived in Brahan Castle near Dingwall, Scotland. When the earl's wife was concerned that her husband was nearly half a year late returning from a trip to Paris, she inquired of his whereabouts from Mackenzie. When he told her that he had a vision of the earl in the arms of another woman, she did not believe him and became so enraged that she ordered that he be burned at the stake. When his execution date was decided, Mackenzie uttered the Seaforth Curse against her family, for which he became famous. The earl, knowing that Mackenzie was correct, tried to stop the execution unsuccessfully. First, Mackenzie stated, "The last of his house [the earl's] would be both deaf and dumb. Also, he would be the father of four sons, all of which he would follow to the tomb." The earl became deaf and mute in 1793, supposedly after the untimely death of his four sons, as predicted.

Second, he stated, "There shall be four great lards [lords], Gairloch, Chisholm, Grant, and Raasay, of whom one will be bucktoothed, another harelipped, another half-witted, and the fourth a stammerer. Chiefs distinguished by these personal marks shall be the allies and neighbors of the last Seaforth." As predicted, Gairloch was bucktoothed, Chisholm had a harelip, Grant was retarded, and Macleod of the House of Raasay stuttered.

Third, he said, "The remnants of his possessions (the earl's) shall be inherited by a white-coifed lassie from the east, and she is to kill her sister." The final heir to the estate had traveled to India with her husband. After he died, she wore the widow's white cap. One day, when she was driving a carriage with her sister, the vehicle overturned and her sister was killed. The accuracy of these predictions is astounding!

By 1995, it was believed that the only way that the curse could be lifted would be to destroy the castle and rebuild from new stones, which the new owners did. They waited apprehensively to see if they have pacified the Braham Seer into lifting the curse.

The Yorkshire Witch (born 1884)

Old Mother Shipton was England's' most famous psychic. In 1488, she was born with a hunchback, and as she grew older, her nose and chin became very long and pointed—so much so that she resembled the portraits of witches depicted during that era. During her childhood, she was responsible for chairs and stools marching up and down stairs by themselves and playing with the dishes. This disturbed her mother so much that she gave the child up to be raised by a nurse maid and sought asylum at a convent.

When she attended school, the other children teased her about her deformity, and she got revenge by causing them to be mysteriously pinched, and some were rendered speechless when they were required to recite their lessons. When two gentlemen remarked about her ugliness, one had his collar replaced by a toilet seat, and the other had his hat replaced by a potty-chair.

Mother Shipton soon discovered that she had the gift of prophecy and made her living telling people's fortunes. She foretold that the mayor of York would be stabbed, and indeed he was stabbed to death by thieves that night. She also foretold that the steeple of Trinity Church and Owen Bridge would fall one night. The steeple was blown down in a storm, and the bridge was destroyed by a flood on the same day.

Her most famous prediction was the outbreak of the Black Plague and the Great Fire of London in 1665. She even predicted that men would climb to rooftops to report the direction of the fire, which they did.

She predicted the death of one of Henry VIII's lord chancellors, Cardinal Wolsey. When several of the lords, who were friends with Wolsey, came to visit her to dispute her prediction, she predicted the fate of each of them, even stating that one of them would be beheaded—his body buried in York and his head traveling to France. His head was stolen by family members and taken to France as predicted. Cardinal Wolsey soon died of dysentery as predicted.

Mother Shipton is most famous for a poem supposedly written by her, depicting the future as reported in a book by Charley Hindley in 1862.

Mother Shipton's Prophecy

Carriages without horses will go
And accidents fill the world with woe
Around the world thoughts shall fly
In the twinkling of an eye
Under water men shall walk
Shall ride, shall sleep, shall be seen,
In white, in black, in green
Iron in water shall float
As easy as a wooden boat

The reference to automobiles crashing into one another, communications through wireless means and the Internet, deep-sea divers, submarines, and modern-day ships is amazing. The white and black symbolized the sailors' uniforms, and marines wear green.

In another verse, she seems to have predicted the American Civil War and Abraham Lincoln's death.

The North will rue its wondrous sore,
But the South shall rue it forever more
The time will come, when seas of blood
Shall mingle with another flood

Mother Shipton predicted the exact same time of her death. She invited friends and relatives to see her off, lay down on her bed, and died.

Although she was a witch, she never practiced evil and, to this day, is honored by her countrymen. A monument was erected near the city of York, praising her skills and prophecies.[32]

---

32 Wilson, The Mammoth Book of Prophecies.

Alfred Lord Tennyson (1809–1892)

One of the most accurate predictions of the future was written by the English poet Tennyson in 1842 and could have been a prediction of a future world war.

For I dipped into the future, far as human eye could see; saw the vision of the world, and all the wonder that would be; saw the heavens fill with commerce, argosies of magic sails, pilots of purple twilight, dropping down with costly bales; heard the heavens fill with shouting, and there rained a ghastly dew from the nations' airy navies grappling in the central blue; far along with world-wide whisper of the south-wind rushing warm; with the standards of the peoples plunging through the thunder storm; till the war-drum throbbed no longer, and the battle flags were furled; In the Parliament of man, the Federation of the world.

Saw the heavens fill with commerce … pilots of the purple twilight dropping down with costly bales. [This can be construed as air commerce.]

Heard the heavens filled with shouting, and there rained a ghastly dew; from the nations' airy navies grappling in the central blue. [This could have predicted the air battles and bombs dropped in future wars from aircraft carriers.]

With the standards of the peoples plunging through the thunderstorm; till the war drums throbbed no longer and the battle flags were furled. [This could depict the flags of the different nations involved in the battles.]

In the Parliament of man, the Federation of the world. [This seems to depict a New World government, which will be necessary to survive the turmoil we are now in.]

Jules Verne (1826–1905)

Jules Verne was a nineteenth-century French novelist, whose work would then have been considered as science fiction. But today, so many of these prophecies are facts that Verne must have been a psychic. Verne was two centuries ahead of his time in some of his predictions, many of which have just been applied in the past century.

He foretold the launching of a spaceship to the moon from a location in Florida. The missile he described was the same weight and height as the Apollo moon expedition. The Apollo 9 splashdown occurred in an area 2.5 miles from where Verne's missile supposedly landed. Verne described weightlessness in one of his novels. He even described a satellite orbiting the earth, guided missiles, and helicopters. Verne also predicted motion pictures as well as submarines.

He foresaw the application of electricity to clocks, cooking stoves, lights, and generators. He predicted the international telephone and predicted that newspapers and motion pictures could be sent instantaneously (television and the Internet).

In 1879, Verne described a devastating war employing a poisonous gas (WWI, 1918) and predicted that the German race would be ruled by an evil dictator, who would envision the German people as a master race (Adolf Hitler).

He predicted transformers that would convert energy from waterfalls, rivers, wind, and the sun (electricity). He envisioned cars, buses, trains, and even air travel from Paris to America.

Other predictions include:

- The atomic bomb
- Seaplanes

- Piped-in Music

- The videophone

- Interplanetary communication

- Global climate control

- Food conveyed directly to the home (Will this be next?)

- Advertisements projected onto clouds

- Energy accumulators (batteries)

- Cryogenics

- Computers

- A tunnel from Paris to New York (now being designed)

Science had not yet progressed this far in the 1800s, so many of his predictions were way ahead of his time.[33]

Edgar Cayce—The Healing Prophet (1877–1945)

Edgar Cayce was a nineteenth-century farm boy born in Kentucky. At the age of nine, he dropped out of school. Later in life, when he was in a trance, he diagnosed the ailments of thousands, as if he were an experienced physician. Cayce not only diagnosed their ailments but even prescribed cures, which worked nearly all of the time. Cayce even did predictions for the future of his patients. Once, the mother of a seven-year-old boy asked him to do a reading for her son. Cayce stated that the boy had several previous reincarnations, but he would not do a future prediction for the boy because he knew his life would soon end. Three years later, the mother wrote that her son had fallen through ice on a

---

33 Wigal, Visions of Nostradamus and Other Prophets.

pond. Strangely enough, just before he died, he told his mother, "I'd like you to be my mummy in my next life." When she told him that it may not be possible, he replied, "I'm going to ask God anyway."

Cayce made many predictions of the future. The most famous of which are as follows:

1. Cayce predicted the Russian Revolution of 1917.

2. He predicted the defeat of Hitler and India's independence from England.

3. Cayce predicted that the East Coast, West Coast, and central USA would disappear under the ocean in 1976; this date has long passed, but recent discoveries indicate that a huge landslide is imminent in the Canary Isle. If this happened, it would create a wave two thousand feet high, traveling at 450 miles per hour across the Atlantic. It would be reduced to approximately 145 feet when it hits the East Coast of the United States and will travel twelve miles inland, destroying most of the Atlantic cities. The Great Lakes would empty into the Mississippi Valley, flooding central USA.

— *Other predictions:*

-   The beginning and end of WWI (1914–1918) and WWII (1939–1945)

-   A major tidal wave in the Philippines (1926)

-   The stock market crash would be in 1929

-   The independence of India from the British would be 1948

- Date of Franklin Delano Roosevelt's death would be 1945

- Creation of the independent state of Israel would be in 1948

- Discovery of the Dead Sea Scrolls would be in 1947–1949

- Invention of the laser (1960) and atomic power plants (1950)

- Major hurricanes in Japan (1959, 1967)

- Major earthquakes in California (1906, 1933, 1971, 1989, 1994)

- Date of John F. Kennedy's death would be in 1963

- The start of WWIII (2012)

- China will be a threat to the United States

- The coming of the Antichrist

Many of these predictions have already happened long after his death.

Cayce's most famous prediction was the existence of the lost continent of Atlantis, which supposedly existed from 50,000 to 10,000 BC. Many of his readings from the 1920s to the 1940s told of this highly advanced civilization, which developed aircraft, submarines, and electricity thousands of years ago. True, these had already been developed at the time of his readings; however, he also stated that the Atlantians had some kind of cosmic ray similar to the modern laser, which could be used to transmit power without wires. He also stated that they had atomic power plants. The invention of the laser did not occur until the 1960s, and the use of atomic power did not occur until the 1950s, which was after Cayce's death in 1945!

The Greek philosopher Plato (428–348 BC) stated that the continent of Atlantis had been swallowed up by the sea circa 10,000 BC in a violent volcanic eruption. Hesiod, a Greek poet (circa 800 BC) stated that there were islands located in the Atlantic that were said to be peopled by mortals, to whom the gods had conferred immortality, and were blessed with abundance. An earlier reference to Atlantis was made by the Greek poet Homer, who was estimated to have lived between 850 and 1200 BC. He called it the Phaeacian land. He could have been referring to the ancient city of Phaeacosos on the Island of Crete.

But what happened to Atlantis, and why is there is no surviving evidence? Atlantis was destroyed by a volcanic eruption and disappeared beneath the sea. There would be no trace of their civilization. But why are there no records? Plato describes how Egyptian priests, in conversation with the Greek historian Solon, stated that Atlantis had been a powerful kingdom that had overrun all of the Mediterranean, except Athens.

Cayce's readings indicated that many of the Atlantians fled to Egypt and were responsible for the construction of the great pyramids. He further stated that Atlantian records were buried in Egypt beneath the paws of the Sphinx. Evidently, for some reason, the Atlantians did not want to share their secrets with the rest of the world. Since digging beneath the sphinx is forbidden, we may never learn their secrets; however, recent probes beneath the sphinx indicate a sizable chamber beneath the paws.

How could such an advanced civilization have vanished? We need to remember that all of our advanced inventions have happened within the last one hundred years. Since the Atlantians did not take any of the machinery required to recreate their civilizations with them, they adopted those of the nations they lived in. After a few hundred years, only legends of Atlantis existed, and they were absorbed into the primitive societies.

In 1470 BC, the volcanic island of Thira (Santorini) erupted with enormous violence, blowing out the entire center of the island. This destroyed the highly advanced Minoan Civilization there (3000–1470 BC). The ensuing earthquake and tsunami (tidal wave) also destroyed their civilization at Knossos on Crete seventy-two miles south of Santorini. A huge cloud of ash covered most of Crete. The surrounding crater on Santorini was covered by ash forty to eighty feet thick. We visited Santorini in 1997. As our ship sailed into the center of the crater, we could see that the walls around the crater were over one thousand feet high, and a small Greek village could be seen perched on the top. Excavation on the crater top revealed a highly advanced city, containing buildings up to three stories high with colorful lifelike frescoes painted on the walls and hundreds of beautifully crafted pottery. There have been other volcanic explosions in the past (i.e., Krakatau 1883), which have leveled islands, so the story of Atlantis may not be all fiction. All these predictions were made long before the events occurred, except for Atlantis.[34]

Jeane Dixon (1932–1997)—The Washington Prophet

I was an avid reader of Jeane Dixon when her books were popular in the 1960s. I recall the first book of hers that I purchased and was amazed at the accuracy of some of her predictions.

When Jeane Dixon was a child, her father took her to meet a gypsy fortune-teller, who was camped nearby. When the woman took Jeane's hand, she knew immediately that Jeane would be

---

34   Cayce, Modern Prophet.

given the gift of prophecy, so she gave her a crystal ball. Later when she moved to Washington DC, just before WWII, Jeane used the crystal ball to foretell the futures of many of the statesmen there. The following are some of the most famous prophecies that had been corroborated before they happened.

1. Several weeks before John F. Kennedy's assassination, she tried to get word to the White House that the president should not make the trip to Dallas. She also had a vision that the name of the person that would cause the assassination had the first two letters *O* and *S* in his name (Oswald) and that it would happen on the morning on November 22, 1963!

2. On July 19, 1964, she predicted that Teddy Kennedy should stay out of private airplanes. The next day Teddy was gravely injured in a light aircraft crash.

3. Robert Kennedy would be assassinated (1968).

4. In November 1948, she predicted that China would go Communist and would be our biggest problem. In September 1949, Mao Si Dun declared China to be the Communist People's Republic.

5. In 1945, she predicted that India would be partitioned and independent in two years. On February 20, 1947, it came to pass.

6. In mid-1947, she predicted that Mahatma Gandhi would be assassinated within six months. In January 1948, Gandhi was killed by a religious fanatic, who did not approve of his multicultural tolerance.

7. In 1961, she predicted the suicide of Marilyn Monroe, and within nine months it had occurred.

8. She predicted the plane crash of Dag Hammarskjold in September of the year that it happened.

9. She predicted that Harry Truman would be elected in 1948, against overwhelming odds that favored Dewey.

10. In May of 1953, she predicted that a silver ball would circle the earth. In 1957, Sputnik was launched.

11. She predicted the American race riots of 1963 and 1964.

12. In 1945, she predicted that Franklin D. Roosevelt had only a few months to live.

13. Churchill would not be reelected in 1945 but that he would be elected in 1951.

14. The Korean War would be a stalemate.

15. Stalin would die in 1953 and would be replaced by a man she described as resembling Bulganin.

16. She predicted Nikita Khrushchev would be elected in 1956.

17. She predicted the death of Secretary of State John Foster Dulles in 1959.

18. She predicted the Alaskan earthquake of 1964.

19. She predicted the death of the three Apollo astronauts by fire in a capsule on the ground.

20. President Nixon would be elected president and would be involved in a wiretapping scandal.

21. A pope would be gravely injured in the late twentieth century (Pope John Paul II)

22. She predicted the fall of the Berlin wall.

23. She predicted the assassination attempt on Governor Wallace.

24. She predicted the invention of night vision goggles and shoulder-held surface to air guided missiles. These weapons are now being used.

25. She predicted that all Christian churches will unite under one universal Christian Church.

26. She predicted that the Antichrist will come.

27. The Davis Straits north of Canada will become an American lifeline during World War III. Melting of the polar caps now taking place would make this possible. Shipments of oil and essentials could be made between the East and West Coasts via the Davis Straits.

28. She predicted that major blackouts on the East Coast will happen.

29. China will be a threat to the United States (now happening!)

Again all of these prophecies came true, some long before these events occurred.[35]

---

35 Dixon, A Gift of Prophecy.

Alan Vaughan

Alan Vaughn (born 1936) is a living psychic. Born in 1936, he did not know that he had any psychic powers until 1965, while working with a Ouija board. The Ouija board was very popular in the 1940s. I had one, but I was never able to predict anything. It consisted of a board with the letters of the alphabet on it and a pointer that you placed your hand on, which supposedly pointed to certain letters unassisted and spelled out words. One day, the board predicted that there would be a massive blizzard in the state of New York. As predicted, there was a blizzard on January 31 to February 1, which dropped over one hundred inches of snow on the state. Then the Ouija board caused him to be possessed by a spirit. After he told the spirit to leave, he realized that he had psychic powers. When Vaughan continued to see phantom spirits, he burned the Ouija board.

But not all Ouija board spirits are evil. The September 2010 issue of the *Smithsonian* reported just such an occurrence. On July 8, 1913, Pearl Curran, a typical St. Louis housewife, was trying to conjure up the spirit of her dead father, who had just passed away, using a Ouija board. Suddenly the pointer leaped into action, and a spirit named Patience Worth identified herself by causing Pearl's fingers to move to the letters on the board. Patience described herself as first living in Portshire, England, in the second half of the seventeenth century. Pearl said she had visions of Patience as a pretty redheaded woman with large brown eyes, who loved to ride horses, and Pearl could see large ships in the background. Patience went on to say that she had later moved to America and was killed by Indians on Nantucket Island.

Pearl and her husband traveled throughout the country, giving performances starring Patience Worth. During the years from 1913 to 1937, Patience produced seven novels, poetry, short stories, and plays and even wrote them simultaneously sometimes. One woman recorded that Patience was capable of dictating 1,500 words an hour. Her poems were among the most published of that time, and the *New York Times* reported her first novel as a work of genius. The Joint Committee of Literary Arts of New York named Patience one of the nation's most outstanding authors.

But all the publicity stirred up distrust. At the time, the noted psychic Harry Houdini and Walter Price were traveling throughout the country, exposing fake mediums. Price spent several weeks interviewing Pearl and her friends and relatives and sitting in on long sessions in which Pearl conjured up Patience. He published a five-hundred-page book concluding that no evidence exists that Pearl had ever produced any Patience Worth material, either consciously or unconsciously. That same cause operating through, but not in Mrs. Curran, must be acknowledged.

The Curran's income dwindled as their reputation became less popular, and after her husband died at the age of fifty-one, Pearly found herself with two small children to raise. Two additional marriages were unsuccessful. She appeared at small gatherings of the movie stars and private parties until her death at the age of fifty-four in 1937. Patience did not desert her until after her death.

Modern-day neuroscientists have tried to explain her ability as being a savant. That is, a person who is mentally retarded but displays genius in one area. But people with ordinary intelligences, who display prodigious feats of memory, are rare, such as Patience, who had a remarkable memory of custom clothing, plants, and cuisine of several historical periods.

Because of Vaughn's psychic abilities, he was awarded a grant from the Parapsychology Foundation of Europe. He organized a group of psychics in an effort to record their prophetic abilities. To their surprise, they found out that he was their best subject. They correctly predicted the number of children he would have and that he would make appearances on television. In 1968, the Central Premonitions Registry was established, which recorded all of the predictions sent in. Vaughan predicted that Robert Kennedy would be shot two weeks before it occurred in memos to his associates. Vaughan dreamed about Martin Luther King's assassination before it happened and recorded it. He also correctly predicted and recorded that enormous scandals in the Nixon administration would occur during the second half of his administration (the Watergate scandal).

Vaughan correctly recorded in December of 1969 that severe flooding would occur on the East Coast of the United States. In June 1972, Hurricane Agnes caused one of the worst floods in US history to the East Coast.

In December 1969, he predicted that a madman would attack the Pope in an attempt to kill him the following year. In November 1970, the Pope was stabbed by a person described as a "madman."

In 1982, Vaughan predicted that a space shuttle launch would have a severe malfunction that could affect the space program. In January of 1986, the Challenger burned up during reentry due to a damaged tile, delaying the shuttle program for three years.

In April of 1993, he predicted that a demonstration against Russian Prime Minister Boris Yeltsin would cause his downfall. In 2001, Yeltsin was ousted after a demonstration, and Mikhail Gorbachev replaced him.

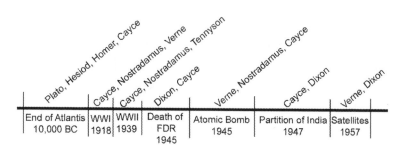

Visions of the Prophets

In January of 1997, Vaughan predicted that the Mars probe would stop transmitting soon after it approached the planet on July 4. In the first week of July, it quit transmitting.

In 1980, he predicted that nuclear weapons would be outlawed in the United States and USSR. In 1997, nuclear disarmament began in earnest.

In 1983, using only his psychic powers, Vaughan was able to disintegrate one patient's kidney stones and another's gallstones. X-rays before and after corroborated that the stones had disappeared.

As far as the future is concerned, Vaughn does not believe that the earth will experience massive destruction in the near future as so many others have.[36]

Mental Telepathy and Psychokinesis

Mental telepathy involves the transmission of messages from one person to another through the use of thoughts only. Psychokinesis involves the movement of objects solely with one's mind. Early investigation by the Society for Physical Research in England found considerable evidence suggesting that mental telepathy and psychokinesis exist.

---

36   Wigal, Visions of Nostradamus and Other Prophets.

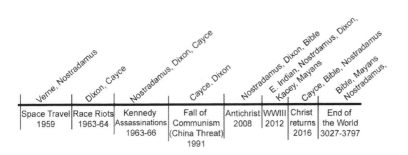

Space Travel 1959	Race Riots 1963-64	Kennedy Assassinations 1963-66	Fall of Communism (China Threat) 1991	Antichrist 2008	WWIII 2012	Christ returns 2016	End of the World 3027-3797

In the United States, the Parapsychology Laboratory at Duke University performed research using cards with designs of stars, circles, pluses, squares, and wavy lines printed on them, which could only be seen by one of the participants. The success of naming the designs on the cards correctly was found to be way beyond probability, proving that such ability does exist. Also, in Duke's experiments on psychokinesis, dice were thrown. Before throwing the dice, the person throwing them informed the investigators the numbers of the dice that would appear upward. The results attained could not be attributed to chance, proving the existence of mind over matter.

In the 1960s, an office in Bavaria was being charged with an excessive amount of telephone calls that would have been impossible to have been placed in such a short amount of time. This was before the age of computer dialing. In addition, pictures swung by themselves, a huge filing cabinet moved without help, drawers flew open independently, and pages flew from a desk calendar. Electrical bulbs exploded and twisted themselves out of their sockets. The office was put on a separate generator, but the electrical problems continued. When a young secretary quit, the phenomenon ceased. It was discovered that the secretary was unhappy with her life and job and was the only possible reason for all the disturbances. It is a well-documented fact that young people around the age of puberty can cause such phenomena to occur. When youth leave the room, the abnormal activity ceases. Such phenomena are known as poltergeists.

In the 1970s, a Russian named Uri Geller was seen on television bending objects with only his thoughts.

In 1971, a laboratory worker at a medical center in New York was able to move a bottle of medicine six inches across a table in either direction by solely thinking about moving it. She was able to accomplish this feat while being observed by other scientists. [37]

In his book, Dr. Deepak Chopra described the brain as having "pure energy" driven by the soul. He cites an example of this. A young man had committed suicide. A week later his mother went to his room to pray for her son. At that moment, a toy car continued to move around the room, even after the mother removed the batteries. The car continued to move for three days! His closest sister insisted that her brother's spirit was operating the car. She began to ask her brother's spirit questions, which the car answered correctly by going right for yes and left for no. The whole family witnessed this phenomenon. It is well-known that the brain emits an electrical current to control the body. Could this be the soul? [38]

Remote Viewing

Remote viewing is the ability to view events that are happening at great distances without the aid of any electronic devices. During the cold war, US intelligence employed psychics to spy on the Soviet Union. Their accuracy was so amazing that the United

37 Reader's Digest Book, Unsolved Mysteries of the Past.
38 Chopra, Life After Death.

States spent millions of dollars for this purpose. The psychics described top-secret Soviet experiments that were being performed inside certain buildings that were later corroborated.

Psychics

When I was sixteen years old, I decided to have my future read by a family friend, who was a psychic. She had cured my friend's and my brother's warts by telling them to say certain chants under a full moon. She also predicted that my mother would have another child even though her doctor had told her that this was not possible. Eleven years later, she gave birth to my sister.

During my reading, I asked her if I would be a success in life, and she answered that I would be. I then asked her if I would marry an Italian girl. She hesitated and then replied, "Yes, and she would be of fair completion." My wife's parents came from the area around Venice, and indeed she is of fair complexion.

Recently a friend of mine went to a psychic, who contacted her dead brother. He informed her of the location of several bank accounts, and indeed he had deposited money in those accounts. In another séance, they witnessed hundreds of soldiers, who had been killed in past wars emerging from the wall. The soldiers told them that they had been wandering aimlessly for years and thanked them for showing them the way to the tunnel of light!

In May of 2006, my friend gave me the name of the physic she had been seeing. When I made the phone call for an appointment, she said "Is this Bongiovanni?" before I told her who I was. I had never met the woman, and she did not know anything about me.

As I entered her house, she commented that I should see a doctor about the deteriorating jaw joint problem, which I do have.

She proceeded to tell me several personal things about my family that only we should have known. She told me that there were several spirits present that I had known, who had passed away. She described one who was around frequently who had light hair and wore it in a tight bun (good description of my wife's mother). She went on to describe another spirit, who was very beautiful, had high cheek bones, dimples, a beautiful smile and eyebrows, and loved the color blue. This was a perfect description of my mother! When she said another spirit named Eva was there with her, I was amazed. Eva was my mother's best friend, who died very young in an accident involving a horse. She went on to describe a spirit who was wearing bib overalls. My deceased friend wore them frequently. She then described my deceased aunt, who I was very fond of.

Describing my past incarnation, she stated that I had been a vicar in England, who had died in 1863, and was buried in a village near the Stonehenge. My previous name was Arthur Thomas, and I had been married to a cute redheaded Irish girl named Alicia Brown and that I had waited one hundred years to be reincarnated until Alicia was reincarnated as my wife, Doris, so that I could remarry her. And just as my first psychic predicted, she is of fair complexion. As I left her house, she mentioned that I should take care of my right leg. There was no way of her knowing that I had accidently cut it that week since I was not limping.

Recently, my sister had a revealing visit to a psychic. As she greeted the psychic, she told my sister that our brother died due to a bad combination of prescription medicines. She had not yet asked the question to the psychic. Our brother had died in his sleep at the age of sixty with no diagnosis for his death, and it had long been a mystery to us.

In 1898, the psychic Morgan Robertson had a vision of a huge ocean liner sailing through a foggy night in the Atlantic Ocean.

He envisioned that the ship was a thousand feet long and was driven by three of the largest propellers he had ever seen. He saw that it was traveling at twenty-three knots, which was too fast for an Atlantic foggy night. Robertson estimated that a ship that size could carry at least two thousand passengers, and he could see them moving about. Much to his dismay, he saw that the ship only carried twenty-four life boats, not enough to cover one quarter of the passengers. Then he heard a voice telling him that the ship was unsinkable. At that same time, he saw it heading for a huge iceberg, which he sensed it was going to strike. As the ship faded from view, he saw the name Titan. Immediately after, Robertson, a writer by trade, wrote about the vision. He continued that on a voyage in April, the seventy-five-thousand-ton liner sank, the iceberg cutting a long gash below the waterline. Although the ship had nineteen watertight compartments, too many had flooded for it to stay afloat. He heard the screams of the passengers as they struggled to stay afloat.

Fourteen years later, in April of 1912, the largest ship ever built, the SS Titanic, was racing through the Atlantic at twenty-three knots, which at that time was a fast speed for that size ship. It was reported by another that there was an entire field of icebergs directly ahead, but the wireless operator did not relay the information to the first officer, because he was too busy sending messages for the wealthy passengers. At 11:30 PM, the lookout saw a huge iceberg straight ahead about a quarter of a mile away. The first officer ordered that the propellers be put in reverse. Had he not done this, the ship could have easily missed the iceberg, but putting the propellers on reverse caused the ship to turn more slowly and just scrape the iceberg, causing a 330-foot gash past several of the watertight compartments. As the ship slowly sank into the Atlantic, only 711 passengers were saved by a nearby ship. Nearly

1,500 people faced their deaths. The facts that Robertson described about the *Titanic*—the number of passengers, the speed, the small number of lifeboats, the weight of the ship, and that the ship will hit an iceberg in the Atlantic in April, causing a huge gash that will flood many compartments, making the liner sink—could not be a mere coincidence. Even the name he envisioned—the Titan—was remarkable. Surely Robertson had the gift of prophecy.

In 1996, two psychics, Scot Hill and Rosemary Walter, predicted when the terrible attack on September 11, 2001 would occur on their talk show, *Psychic Saturday Night*. They both believed that the attack would occur in 2001, between September and November.

In September 1996, Hill had a dream that Princess Diana would be on the cover of a ladies magazine, which was photographed in Paris; but when he picked up the magazine, a picture of the Eiffel Tower appeared on it instead of Princess Diana. He then realized that Diana wasn't on the cover because she would be killed, and her death was connected to something happening in Paris. Diana was killed in an automobile accident nearly a year later in August of 1997 in Paris.

In a broadcast in 1997, Hill also predicted that the French passenger jet, the Concorde, would explode, causing a terrible loss of life. On July 25, 2000, while the Concorde was taking off from Paris's airport, one of the engines caught fire; and the plane crashed, killing everyone on board.

Another psychic, David Mandel, predicted the 2000 Concorde crash in July 1997. Mandel, an artist, made a picture of the event, took it to the local bank, and had it photographed next to the calendar clock on the bank to prove its authenticity. The picture showed a delta-winged jet on fire and a French flag in one corner of the picture, indicating that the accident would occur in France.

On September 11, 1996, Mandel dreamed that the twin towers were collapsing while flames engulfed them. When he awoke, he drew a picture of the event and took it down to the bank again to be photographed next to the clock for proof of authenticity. Five years later, the towers were completely destroyed, resulting in over three thousand deaths.

In 1990, the security officer for Morgan Stanley, Rick Rescorla, had a premonition that the World Trade Center could easily collapse if a bomb was exploded in the underground parking garage. Rescorla prepared a report and sent it to New York Port Authority with no response.

On February 1993, a bomb hidden in a van located in the underground garage exploded. Although the bomb damaged several of the building's support beams, the building fortunately did not collapse. However, six people were killed and two thousand were injured. If the bomb had been successful, fifty thousand people could have been killed, because without a warning, they could not have been evacuated in time. Rescorla led the evacuation of people from twenty floors of the building and was the last person to leave.

Finally Rescorla convinced the New York Port Authority to increase the building's security. He had a premonition that this time the threat would come from an attack by air. On September 11, 2001, when the first plane hit the north tower, the Port Authority, believing that this was an accidental air crash, told everyone in the south tower to remain where they were. Rescorla, however, told everyone to evacuate the south tower minutes before the second jet hit the south tower. Again he was one of the last persons in the building. This time it cost him his life.[39]

---

39 Wilson, The Mammoth Book of Prophecies.

Near-Death Experiences

A near-death experience can be described as the process of being pronounced dead and returning back to life. Most people experience the same common events during a near-death experience. Usually the person is dying from an illness or accident.

First, the person's heart stops and then they quit breathing. Next, the person feels a sense of well-being and peace. There is no longer any pain. They then find themselves separated from their body floating in the air, looking down on the physician and nurses trying to resuscitate them. In some instances, they can later describe what's happening in other rooms of the hospital and even outside the hospital. One person even described the special instruments that were used for the operation. This would not be possible if they had not left their body! At this point, one begins to realize that they are dead and are surprised that they still have vision, hearing, and are mentally alert. After about ten minutes, they hear themselves are pronounced dead and find themselves in a dark space with a bright light at the end of a tunnel. Upon entering the light, they find themselves in another world of indescribable beauty. Many describe the landscape as being like the Garden of Eden. Some describe buildings with glass walls (heaven?). My brother-in-law described such a light just before he died, and a good friend of mine described this experience after he had a near-death experience.

They are then greeted by a being emitting a brilliant light (angel?) and possibly friends or relatives. They are asked if they would like to return to life, and if they agree, they return to their body and the pain returns.

If one is not sure at this point, they are given a "life review" of everything that has occurred in their life. This is projected in a full-color three-dimensional view, as if one is actually in the scene. One perceives the effect they have had on all the people in their lives and feels the emotions one has had on these people. They feel as if they are reliving their lives, but this happens in an instant.

They are asked again if they would like to return to life. If they still desire not to return to life, they may be told they must return to life because it is not yet their time. Obviously all persons who have had near-death experiences return to life or we would not be hearing these stories.

The people who have had these near-death experiences seem to lose all fear of death because they have experienced that there is a beautiful afterlife. Their lives are forever changed, and their sense of values, attitudes, and behaviors are also changed.[40]

Some physicians have stated that when the hospital lights are dim, they have actually seen the soul leaving the body at the moment of death. One nurse described it as a green glow.

In 1901, a physician named Charles Cullis conducted a study on patients who were near death from tuberculosis. He weighed them just before and just after death and found that they averaged a weight loss of twenty-three grams (.75 ounce). He weighed the patient again after each hour and found that the patient had lost only an additional ounce per hour, which was much slower than the instantaneous weight loss just after death. He determined that the second weight loss was water. Dr. Cullis assumed that the initial weight loss was the weight of the soul upon leaving the body![41]

40   Lundhal and Widdison, The Eternal Journey.
41   Roach, Spook.

Reincarnation

Reincarnation is described as the passing of the soul, after death, into a new body. This belief is strongly accepted in Hinduism and Buddhism but is not practiced in the Christian and Jewish religion. Hinduism and Buddhism believes that the soul will be resurrected until the positive actions of the soul outweigh the negative actions of the past lives (karma), after which it will no longer be required to reincarnate and can remain in heaven.

As previously mentioned, one of the strongest advocates of reincarnation was Edgar Cayce, the healing prophet. In a trance, Cayce (having no medical training) would not only diagnose the ailments of his subject but also prescribed cures, which in many cases were successful. Cayce performed thousands of readings in his lifetime. In many of these, he recalled that he too had lived several previous lives as a citizen of the lost continent of Atlantis, an Egyptian priest, a monk, a friend of the apostle Paul, and a mercenary in the British War of 1752.

Cayce believed that we retain some of our knowledge gained from previous incarnations, and these would be recalled in the next incarnation as talents. He stated that our subconscious contains all the knowledge of the world, of the past and of the future to come (akashic records). If the mind is directed toward beneficial creativity, then resources will be drawn from the subconscious to provide help for performing the tasks.[42]

During his readings, Cayce uncovered the previous lives of many of his patients. They had been doctors, lawyers, and other professionals in their past lives and now continued these occupations. Many of these predictions were proven true. One woman had accompanied the apostle Paul and was a slave in ancient Persia.

---

42 Cayce, The Akashic Records

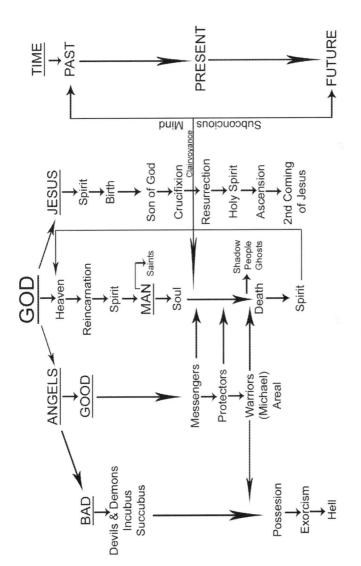

Reincarnation

She had also been a teacher, a dance-hall gambler, and a prostitute in the Old West. In one instance in California, there was a woman named Etta Tetlow, a dance-hall girl. Browsing through old records of the Barbary Coast in San Francisco, she came across an old dance-hall entertainment poster and was shocked when she read the name Tetlow as one of the entertainers. Cayce had correctly predicted that one of her sons would become a lawyer.

Cayce also did readings for babies. One baby girl had been a singer and a dancer in ancient Greece and an entertainer for one of the early kings of France. When she reached adulthood, she loved flowing Grecian gowns and French perfumes. He recalled how her ancestors had been citizens of Atlantis. She went on to become a recognized ballet dancer.

One reading recalled that a baby boy had been a physician and farmer in a previous life. The young man later became a psychologist and loved working on his uncle's farm.

One woman was fascinated by circuses but fled in panic when they brought in the lions. Cayce, not knowing of this fear, had told her she had been one of the Christians in early Rome that had been fed to the lions.

One WWII soldier, passing through Bavaria, suddenly saw himself as a crusader in that country. He later remembered that Cayce has predicted that he was a crusader in a previous life.

Child prodigies are perfect examples of carrying talents from previous incarnations. Mozart, at age five, produced music of a genius. Josef Hoffman played the piano at two and half. A six-year-old Turkish boy produced artwork exhibited in the art galleries of Europe without even a painting lesson. Amazingly his favorite subject was cowboys of the Old West even though he has never visited the Old West.

Many of Cayce's readings told some parents that their babies had been architects, tailors, and doctors and correctly predicted that they would become architects, tailors, and doctors when they reach adulthood, because these aptitudes had been brought over from previous lives.

One young man remembered in vivid detail that he had died in a submarine attack during WWII. When he checked it out, he found it to be true. When he visited his past life's home, he had a feeling of déjà vu.

Another five-year-old boy had a passion for WWII Corsair airplanes (the ones with the gull wings). He insisted that he had been a WWII pilot, who had been shot down on Iwo Jima, an island in the Pacific. He described the battle in such detail that his parents checked it out and found it to be true! He remembered his name as a pilot and the name of others in the battle. Survivors of the battle corroborated that a pilot with that name had been shot down during the battle of Iwo Jima.[43]

Do souls have memory? American physician Ian Stevenson, of the University of Virginia, studied several hundred cases. Of these, twenty of the findings were proven to be true beyond a doubt. The investigations were performed on children between the ages of two and four, because after that age, the children can no longer remember their past lives. It is believed that before the age of five, the reincarnated soul is still getting use to its new body and can still remember its past life.

Most of these reincarnations occur shortly after the violent death of an individual. The children remembered how many children they had and their previous residences, although they had never visited the town where they have lived in their previous incarnation. They remembered the names of relatives and their

43 Cayce, Modern Prophet.

previous spouses, previous parents' names from photographs, previous occupations, and how they died. One child in India even remembered where he had hidden valuables during a previous life period. In India, reincarnation is viewed as a normal event since it is part of their religion. Some children carry fears from their past lives. They often describe being shot or mutilated with amazing accuracy and then bear the scars of the deceased person, who has been reincarnated.

The early Christian Church believed in reincarnation until the sixth century AD, when it was declared heresy by the Second Council of Constantinople because they felt that this would give one too much time to strive for salvation.

Many of the children described having to wait at different locations before crossing over into heaven. They were then given choices about their next life (e.g., choosing a new family and a new profession). Once in heaven, they were given an occupation until they returned to their new life.

A psychic friend of mine related that she and her sister had been pecked to death by birds while on a wagon train heading for California in the Old West. She now has a fear of birds. Also, she had followed a popular singer all over the country to hear his concerts for some unknown reason. She later found out that she had been married to him in a previous life.

Another friend of mine visited Russia for the first time. When he arrived at a certain city, he had such a strong feeling that something profound was going to happen that he nearly fainted. Later when he walked through the city, he somehow knew directions to all the streets without consulting a map. His companions were amazed. Could he have lived there in a previous life?

Astral Travel

Astral travel is when the sprit leaves the body and can travel anywhere in the universe. The spirit can meet other astral travelers on its journey. Out-of-body projections are common in near-death experiences. The astral body is connected to the physical body by an infinitely stretchable silver-colored cord. Sometimes astral travel is experienced during dreams. I had such an experience at the time of my grandfather's death. I found myself floating up and down the stairs in his house, and I ended up in a shallow grave in his front yard while pulling dirt on myself. My youngest son has also had an out-of-body experience as well as one of my coworkers.

Some astral travelers had the experience of traveling through outer space at the speed of light, past the limit of the solar system. Galaxies appeared and then disappeared as a mere point of light. Some astral travelers have been pronounced dead for up to an hour and, when they returned, showed no ill effects.

Exorcism

Exorcism involves the right of expelling the devil or his demons from victims who have been possessed by them. The Catholic Church and some Protestant churches practice exorcism. In some instances, there may be more than one demon possessing a person. One such instance occurred when Jesus performed an exorcism on a crazed man in the land of Gerasenes. The demon caused the man to become so powerful that not even chains could bind him. He lived in caves, cut into the mountain like a wild animal, yelling and cutting himself with sharp objects. Jesus, seeing that he was possessed, cried out to the demons to reveal their names. The demons cried out, "My name is Legion, for we are many." Jesus demanded that they leave the man. They pleaded with him not to send them back to hell, so he placed them in a nearby heard of swine that were so frightened they jumped into the sea and drowned.

The Catholic Church has a detailed rite for performing exorcism. The ritual of Canon Law allows authorized priests to perform exorcism, not only over Christians, but also over anyone outside the church. The greatest danger to the exorcist is that the priest may become possessed by the demons himself.

During the exorcism, salt (representing purity), wine (representing the blood of Christ), a crucifix, holy water, and relics of the saints are used while the priest recites the ritual.

Father Jean Siren, a Jesuit exorcist of Loudin, France, became possessed while attempting to perform an exorcism on Sister Jeannes des Angst. Afterward, he experienced severe muscle pain, which caused him poor health and mental problems for the rest of his life.

The place where the exorcism should be performed should be where there is a definite connection between the demon and the victim. Three people usually assist the exorcist—a young priest, a physician, and a member of the family.

The following procedures should be followed during the exorcism:

1. When the exorcist becomes aware of the demon's presence, he must determine its name. After the demon realizes that he has been exposed, complete chaos occurs, such as verbal obscenities, frightening visions, loud noises, and foul odors. The demon then turns on the victim.

2. The demon's voice then becomes an unintelligibly distressed babble, and he must be silenced before the exorcism can continue.

3. As the ritual continues, the exorcist feels direct contact with the entity. The priest tries to obtain more information from the demon so he can more easily be expelled. It does not want to leave, because it will then have to return to hell.

4. The priest demands that the demon leave in the name of Jesus Christ. The entity hopefully leaves, and its ranting becomes more distant.

5. The miracle of exorcism throughout history provides strong proof that the devil and his demons are possessing people.

The most famous exorcism occurred in Washington DC and Saint Louis, Missouri, in 1949. The possession of a young boy started in a suburb of Washington DC and inspired the book and movie *The Exorcist*. Initially, bedsheets and blankets were torn from his bed by an unseen entity. A rabbi was summoned when the demon began speaking in the Hebrew (Aramaic) language, the language spoken by Jesus. While the boy was sleeping in a heavy armchair, it was slammed against the wall. While sleeping on the floor, he was carried under the bed by some unknown force. Bloody scratches appeared on the boy's body, spelling obscene words. A priest was summoned when the boy began to speak in Latin. Although the boy was then taken to his mother's home in Saint Louis, scratched words continued to appear on him, objects flew across the room, and a chair he was sitting on spun out of control. After the boy was baptized, he flew into a rage. During the exorcism, the priest demanded that the demon reveal itself. Obscene words, including "hell," were scratched on the boy; his voice changed, and he vomited on the priests face. The priest's exorcism manual was then vaporized. A voice identifying itself as Michael, the archangel, ordered the demon to depart. The boy's body shook violently and then became calm. The boy exclaimed, "He is gone." The exorcism had finally worked. Forty-one witnesses signed a document stating that the paranormal event was indeed true. Over three hundred possession cases were reported in New York City in 1989–1995. Ten exorcisms were successfully performed.[44]

A highly respected pastor and friend of mine witnessed the exiting of a demon while he was performing an exorcism. The demon left the individual and took the shape of a ball of energy, similar to St. Elmo's light. The entity rose to the ceiling and followed a chain holding a vine down to a plant and destroyed it. Ten people in the congregation witnessed the event in amazement, which leaves no doubt to the validity of the occurrence.

---

44 Wikipedia.

CHAPTER V

Ghosts

Personal Experiences

Do the dead see us? The Bible says nothing of ghosts, but the visiting ghosts of relatives and those from other periods of history seem to indicate that they do. I have talked to several friends and relatives who have actually seen ghosts. My oldest son has a video of one. Ghost hunters have many photographs of them. A close friend and her husband saw the ghost of his mother in her bedroom. Before her husband died, he told her that he had been followed around by a small apparition, and just before he died, a tall one followed him around. Another friend of mine told me that she had seen the ghost of her husband on the eve of his death.

My youngest son has ghosts in his turn-of-the-twentieth-century Victorian home. Several times he has heard footsteps on the stairs, but when he comes downstairs to investigate, no one is there. He finally told the entity to stop, and it did! He also saw the apparition of a beautiful woman with long blonde curls dressed in a Victorian dress standing on the stairs. Another time, my son had made plans for remodeling his kitchen and hung them on the refrigerator. The next day, he found the plans torn up on the floor. This happened again when he redrew the plans. The third time it happened, he was very angry and told the entity to quit tearing up the plans, that he was only making improvements. It never happened again.

Recently my brother-in-law stayed at a century-old inn. That evening he saw the ghost of a man with a handlebar mustache in his bedroom, dressed in clothing of that period. The next day, he told the innkeeper what he had seen. The innkeeper confirmed that there had been several other sightings of that ghost.

Types of Ghosts

There are four types of ghosts.

The first is related to an intense happening in the past, such as a killing or a battle. The event replays itself out like one is looking at a motion picture with no interaction between you and the event. The event is usually triggered by someone who is a good receptor. This type of haunting presents no danger to the witnesses.

The second type is an actual apparition. You may hear voices, music, footsteps, and smell odor with no sources or see mists or strange lights. You may feel coldness or touches. This type is the spirit of a deceased person, who remains Earth-bound because of a tragic death, the fear of leaving, or because the spirit has some unfinished business. The spirit may remain until it is able to pass on a message. The spirit may try to get attention by turning lights on and off, moving items, or making noises. A friend of mine had electrical plugs removed, which were behind furniture, by some unknown force after her husband had passed away. This type of haunting is usually harmless.

The third type of ghost is actually a demon. These are potentially dangerous and could harm you. They often appear when practicing séances, playing with Ouija boards, practicing black magic, or practicing satanic worship. Contacting this type of spirit could result in bodily harm or even demonic possession.

The fourth type of ghost is known as a poltergeist. This ghost can cause knocking, voices, smells, apparitions, and even furniture flying around on its own. Poltergeists usually appear when a person going through puberty is in the room. It is believed that this person's subconscious mind is causing all this activity, and they are not even aware of it. When this person leaves the room, this activity ceases. This is not a human spirit and is usually harmless.

Again, this is proof of the power of mind over matter.

Why Some Spirits Remain on Earth

Some spirits remain earth-bound because they have not found their way to the tunnel of light into the next world. They account for many hauntings.

Some remain near the site of their deaths, especially if their deaths were unexpected. They don't realize that they have died and try to make contact with anyone who is a good receptor.

Some sprits remain because they fear what will happen after they pass through the tunnel of light. Will their existences end? Will they go to hell? Will they be punished for their bad deeds?

Some remain on earth because of unfinished business. They may try to contact someone in order to accomplish this. Once they have completed their tasks, they usually pass on.

Suicide victims remain behind because they feel guilty, especially if they leave loved ones behind who are uncared for.

If the survivors have difficulty letting go of the deceased, their spirits will remain Earth-bound until the living finish their grieving.[45]

---

45 Wikipedia, The Free Encyclopedia

CHAPTER VI

Heaven

Is there a divine paradise that awaits me when I die? I have spent years pondering this question. For me, the existence of heaven means that the soul survives the death of the body and becomes the spirit which lives forever in heaven.

Description of Heaven

In her book, Rene Pache describes heaven and quotes the Bible as her source. The apostle Paul was carried up into heaven and described it in "unspeakable words which is unlawful for a man to utter." In other words, it was indescribable in earthly terms since he had never seen anything like it on earth (2 Cor. 12:4).[46]

The apostle John of Patimas is given a glimpse of heaven and describes it in earthly terms in Revelation 21:10–27. He calls it the New Jerusalem and describes it as a city surrounded by a wall of Jasper (transparent marble) 230 feet high to prevent the disbelievers from entering. The city is protected by a transparent

---

46 Pache, The Future Life.

cube, 1,500 miles on each side. Can you imagine a city stretching from Kansas City to New York and from New Orleans to the Canadian border, rising 1,500 miles into the clouds, way beyond the height of the satellites orbiting the earth? The city will be like a greenhouse since the atmosphere outside of the cube will be polluted. There are twelve gates in the wall, each resembling a giant pearl, signifying the twelve tribes of Israel. Each gate is guarded by an angel (probably cherubim with flaming swords) similar to those that guarded the Garden of Eden. There will be twelve foundations named after the twelve apostles. He goes on to describe that the streets are of gold (probably shone like gold to him) and the buildings are transparent like glass (sounds like our modern skyscrapers). There is no need for the sun since the whole city shines like crystal (obviously some new kind of lighting still unknown to man or could be electric lighting). The countryside would be comparable to the Garden of Eden. Could heaven be the Garden of Eden with the river of life flowing from the throne of God? The tree of life grows on each side of the river, which yields fruit every month, and the leaves of the tree assure perpetual health (apparently an herbal medicine). Near-death experiences give similar descriptions. The Epistle to the Hebrews hints that the New Jerusalem will be near Mount Zion. If so, then it will stretch the entire length of the Mediterranean to the west or as far as China to the east!

Jesus said, "In my father's house, there are many mansions ... I go to prepare a place for you." He is indicating that there are places for all in heaven. It recalls to mind the story of a miser, who was walking down the heavenly streets, remarking how beautiful the mansions were. Then he came to a single-room house and remarked to his angelic guide, "Why are all the mansions so huge except for this small house?" The angel replied, "This is your house, for this is all you deserved for your miserly contributions to charity."

In his book, Yogi Yogananda describes how his guru, Sri Yukteswar died, went to heaven, and returned. He described heaven as another universe much grander than ours. Each sun has its own astral planets, not void of life like most of ours. The inhabitants use beams of light to travel from one planet to another at the speed of light.

The astral planets are beautiful, clean, pure, and devoid of all the pollution that we have created here. They maintain constant spring-like temperature and contain beautiful lakes, seas, rivers, and a myriad of fish and animals. Trees produce any fruit desired.

The astral body resembles our body on earth but of a person in one's youth. This would explain why the apostles did not recognize Jesus after his resurrection. He appeared much younger, but they did recognize his voice.

Injuries are healed instantly. Friends and relatives will recognize each other and the heavenly residents work out problems of cosmic government and their redemption of earth-bound souls. Communication is by mental telepathy. This agrees with observations from near-death experiences, that angels communicate with their minds or telepathy. Life spans are from five hundred to one thousand years there. The astral world is also free from diseases.

Each individual must undergo many reincarnations in order to obtain his final freedom, at which time he will be free to choose to remain in the astral cosmic or return to earth to help other souls return to heaven. Persons must continue to reincarnate until they have repaid their karmic debts (required earthly achievements).[47]

47 Yogananda, Autobiography of a Yogi.

Professor Gary Schwartz of the University of Arizona has been performing studies of several noted psychics regarding what the afterlife is like. The psychics asked several questions of known dead persons and received some remarkable answers. The psychics informed him that the dead communicate with mental telepathy—that is, through thoughts, not speech. Fifty percent of them replied that they ate, but there were no obese people in heaven. The replies to these questions imply that they do have bodies and can choose what body they desire. One person who was obviously obese in life replied that they could wear pleated pants now in heaven. The psychics were told that the weather was warm all the time, and the humidity was low, indicating again that they must have bodies in order to sense heat. One replied that they have music and played a few chords, showing that they have a sense of hearing. There are angels in heaven, buy they do not associate with the dead. Angels perform important duties. When they were asked if there was sex in heaven, they replied that it was possible. However, there would be no need for intercourse for procreation, because people existed forever. One even stated that they have X-ray vision and can even see through skin. They can read each other's thoughts. There are no illnesses, no housing, you own nothing, and have no worries. One replied that they rely on our activities for some of their amusement and grow bored when we sleep. They have friends, books, and can smell the flowers all year-round because the flowers never die, indicating that they have a sense of smell. Sailing is one of the pastimes. High-level managers and accountants are needed in heaven. This indicates to me that they have some sort of structured government. Doctors are not needed, because there are no diseases or infirmaries. One went on to describe the countryside as being like the Garden of Eden, with peaceful lakes, rivers, and seas with boats of all kinds.

The residents can travel very fast by thought alone. This would sure beat the security lines at the airports. The most important information that they conveyed was that we keep our own personalities. This implies that the soul does keep its memory and does carry it beyond the grave![48]

Our Duties in Heaven

In her book, René Pache describes heaven as stated in the Bible.

In heaven, the search and achievement of knowledge will be unsurpassed. There will be no more unanswered questions, no more ignorance, and no more mistakes. At last we will have answers to all the whys.

The Bible tells us that in heaven we will finally learn to love and understand each other, and we will all be united. "He who has begun a just work will perfect it" (Phil. 1:6).

Heaven will be a place of perfect love. Our souls will be completely comforted. There will no longer be sorrow. There will be no more hurrying, delays, wasting of time; no more sickness, death, pain, hunger, and thirst. There will be no more sense of time—only eternity! We will be reunited with our loved ones in heaven and shall make new acquaintances. All the apostles and prophets of the Bible will be recognized there.

There will be no need for procreation in heaven since we will live for eternity. Will we be bored in heaven? Although much time will be spent in the adoration of God, it will be a time of love.

We will work without fatigue or error on our favorite projects.

After Jesus's second coming he will rule the earth for one thousand years, and there will be peace.

---

48 Schwartz, The Afterlife.

Those who want to go to heaven will go there, and just as surely, those who want to go with the devil will also have their choice after having been deceived by his promises.[49]

As I have researched these speculations about heaven, I have come to some personal conclusions. The aspects of heaven that I find fascinating and comforting are that we finally understand the true meaning of love and happiness. We will never be bored. Our work and education will continue. But at the same time, there are aspects of heaven that disturb me and simply do not make sense to me, such as the apostle John's description of heaven as being a walled fortress surrounded by a glass cube, 1,500 miles square, and guarded by angels with flaming swords. Why would heaven need guarded walls if all the evil persons are in hell? He seems to be describing the walls of Jerusalem, which were needed at his time to prevent invasions.

---

49   Pache, The Future Life.

Summary and Conclusions

Summary

As I wrote this book, I have tried to imagine the readers as truth seekers like myself, raised in the era of scientific materialism yet longing for some part of the religious, paranormal, and miraculous stories to be objectively and verifiably the truth. In some ways, this book has been about me, about my fears and hopes, and about the ways in which I convince myself to believe in the seemingly unbelievable.

There are some high points of this journey that stand out in my mind.

Genesis agrees remarkably with the sequence in which plants, fish, birds, animals, and man were created that science relates. Moses could not have written it without the help of God, because how could he have known this sequence?

The Garden of Eden is described in several other ancient texts besides the Bible. The Bible locates it in Armenia.

We all have certain talents, which only could have been acquired in a previous life. Our purpose in life is to further develop these talents for the good of others.

God has given us a soul and freedom to choose how we will use our life.

Several prophets of the Bible have similar visions of God:

- That he has the likeness of a man

- That he glowed like incandescent light

- That he sat on a throne issuing fiery flames and sounded like the roar of the ocean

Archeological evidence and written evidence (other than the Bible) of a great flood has been found in the Tigress-Euphrates valley. Remains of a huge ark have been spotted on Mount Ararat.

The remains of two burned cities and humans, dating back to circa 2500 BC and found near the southern end of the Dead Sea, could be those of Sodom and Gomorrah.

Written evidence other than the Bible corroborates the story of the Exodus and Joshua's conquest of Palestine. Archeological evidence also shows that several of these cities mentioned in the Bible had been destroyed by fire at that time.

All of the places mentioned in the New Testament, such as where Jesus gave his sermons and where he was crucified, can be identified today. All of the Old Testament prophecies concerning Jesus's birth, ministries, and crucifixion had come to pass. Ancient texts other than the Bible describe Jesus and his ministries.

Many of the miracles and healing power of the saints have been witnessed by noted physicians and fully documented. The miracles of Fatima and Lourdes have been witnessed by thousands.

Appearances of angels as guardians have been documented in police records and throughout history.

Possession by Satan and his demons have been witnessed during exorcisms.

Precognition, or the ability to predict the future, has been exhibited by prophets of the past and modern prophets and seems to indicate that many major events have already been planned. Many of the prophets had predicted the same events although they lived at different times in the past. Modern-day and past prophets are predicting World War III by 2012.

Mental telepathy indicates that the mind has a sixth sense, which we developed in the Stone Age to warn us of dangers and lost when we became civilized.

Near-death experiences give us a glimpse of what heaven will be like as the soul leaves the body after death.

Hinduism and Buddhism believe that the soul will be reincarnated into a new body after death. Past-life regressions under hypnosis have been proven true in many instances.

The occurrence of child prodigies seems to indicate our talents acquired during past lives have been retained in some cases.

Visitations from ghosts seem to indicate that another astral plane exists and proves the existence of the soul.

The apostles Paul and John were given a glimpse of heaven. John describes it in great detail in Revelation 21:10–27 as being like the Garden of Eden.

In heaven, we will work without fatigue on our favorite projects.

Conclusions

Archeological and ancient written evidence (other than the Bible) shows that the stories in the Bible are true, and if so, the existence of a creator and heaven as told in the Bible must also be true. Ancient texts (other than the Bible) describe Jesus and his ministries, so his existence must also be true.

The miracles and healing powers of the saints and the miracles of Fatima and Lourdes have been fully authenticated and witnessed by thousands. This indicates that they were tapping into some unearthly power from another astral plane (heaven).

Documented appearances of angels and possession of demons offer proof of the existence of heaven and hell.

The ability to predict the future is proof that there is some divine power that plans future events.

Near-death experiences offer proof that heaven and souls do indeed exist after death.

Visitations from ghosts show that we possess souls, and they may remain on Earth after death.

The description of heaven given by John in Revelation describes heaven like a modern-day city and the countryside like the Garden of Eden. How would he know what a modern-day city looked like in the first century without having seen it?

The Old Testament prophets and Jesus spoke of heaven and hell many times in the Bible. Since the stories in the Bible can be proven through written and archeological evidence, then the existence of heaven and hell must also be true.

All of this offers proof (at least to me) that a creator, Jesus Christ, angels and demons, the soul, and heaven do exist!

This is my case for heaven.

Bibliography

Benavides, Rudolfo. *Dramatic Prophecies of the Great Pyramids.* SA, Mexico: Editores Mexicanos Unidos, 1969.

Blackmore, Susan. *Consciousness: An Introduction.* Oxford University Press, 2004.

Bowman, Carol. *Children's Past Lives.* Bantam, 1998.

Carter, Mary Ellen. *Edgar Cayce: Modern Prophet.* Gramercy Books, 1967–1989.

Cayce, Edgar, Gail Schwartzer, and Douglas G. Richards. *Mysteries of Atlantis Revisited: The Century's Greatest Psychic Confronts One of the World's Oldest Mysteries.* Harper and Row, 1988.

Chahin, M. *The Kingdom of Armenia.* Dorset Press, 1991.

Cheetam, Erika. *The Final Prophecies of Nostradamus.* Futural, 1990.

Chopra, Deepak. *Life after Death.* Harmony Books, 2006.

Coward, Harold. *Life after Death in World Religions.* Orbis, 1997.

Cuxhead, Nona. *Mindpower.* Penguin, 1976.

Drolma, Delog Dawa. *Journey into the Realms Beyond Death*. Padme Publishing, 1995.

Dixon, Jeane. *My Life and Prophecies*. G.K. Hall, 1971.

Friede, Eleanor. *The Awakened Mind*. Delacorte Press, 1979.

Furst, Jeffrey. *Edgar Cayce's Story of Jesus*. Berkley Books, 1926.

Gibson, Arvin S. *Echoes from Eternity: New Near-Death Experiences*. Horizon Publishing,   1993.

Gibson, Michael. *Follow Me: A Journey with Jesus*. Morris Publishing, 1996.

Grant, Michael. *The Ancient Historians*. Barnes and Noble, 1994.

Grey, Margot. *Return from Death*. Arkana Publishing, 1985.

Grun, Bernard. *The Timetables of History*. Simon and Schuster, 1982.

Halberstam, Yitta, and Judith Leventhal. *Small Miracles*. Adams Media Corporation, 1998.

Halley, Henry H. *Halley's Bible Handbook*. Zundervan Publishing, 1963.

Heinerman, Joseph. *Spirit World Manifestations*. Utah Magazine Printing and Publishing, 1978.

Hinze, Sarah. *Life before Life*. Cedar Fort Inc., 1993.

Hogue, John. *Nostradamus and the Millennium*. Doubleday, 1987.

King, Francis. *Nostradamus: Prophecies Fulfilled*. Saint Martin's Press, 1994.

King James Version "The Holy Bible"

King, Ursala. *Christian Mystics*. Simon and Schuster, 1998.

LaViolette, Paul A. *Earth under Fire*. Bear and Company, 2005.

LeVert, Liberte. *The Prophecies and Enigmas of Nostradamus*. Glen Rock, 1997.

Levy, David. *Skywatching*. Time Life Books, 1998.

Lundhal, Craig R., and Harold A. Widdison. *The Eternal Journey*. Warner Books, Inc., 1997.

Maclean, Dorothy. *To Hear the Angels Sing*. Lindisfarne Books, 1994.

Mahara, Nisargoft. *I Am That*. Acorn Press, 1990.

Moody, Raymond. *Life after Life*. Mocking Bird Books, 1975.

Montgomery, Ruth. *A Gift of Prophecy*. Bantam Books, 1966.

Morse, Melvin. *Closer to the Light*. Ivy Books, 1990.

Nulnad, Sherman B. *How We Die: Reflections on Life's Final Chapter*. Knopf, 1994.

Pache, Rene. *The Future Life*. Moody Press, 1962.

Pagels, Elaine . *The Gnostic Gospels*. Vintage, 1989.

Pagels, Elaine. *The Origin of Satan*. Vantage, 1996.

Pauls, Stefan. *Nostradamus 1999: Who Will Survive*. Saint Paul, 1977.

Pearce, Joseph Clinton. *The Biology of Transcendence*. Park Street Press, 2002.

Perkins, James. *Experiencing Reincarnation*. Theosophical Publishing House, 1977.

Pubos, Allison. *Don't Kiss Them Good-bye*. Fireside, 2005.

Reader's Digest. *Unsolved Mysteries of the Past (Quest for the Unknown)*. Reader's Digest Association, Inc. 1991.

Roach, Mary. *Spook: Science Tackles the Afterlife*. WW Norton, 2005.

Sanford, Joshua. *Healing and Wholeness*. Doubleday, 1966.

Schwartz, Gary. *The Afterlife*. Atri Books, 2003.

Sherwood, Ben. *The Survivors Club*. Grand Central Publishing, 2009.

Smith, Carol. *Everyday Guide to the Bible*. Humble Creek Publishing, 1995.

Smith, Carol. *The Everyday Guide to Prophecy*. Humble Creek, 2005.

Stearn, Jess. *The Sleeping Prophet*. Bantam Books, 1968.

Steigar, Brad and Sherry. *Miracles of Healing*. Adams Media, 2004.

The Catholic Encyclopedia http://www.newadvent.org/cathern/

The Nostradamus Code: World War III. Truth Revealed Publishing, 2005.

Thuston, Mark A. *Visions and Prophecies for a New Age*. A.R.E. Press, 1981.

Todeschi, Kevin J., *"Edgar Cayce on the Akashic Records"*, A.R.E. Press, 1998

Treece, Patricia. *Nothing Short of a Miracle: The Healing Power of the Saints*. Doubleday, 1988.

Trunga, Chogyam. *Cutting through Spiritual Materialism*. Chambhala, 2002.

Turner, Alice. *The History of Hell*. Harvest, 1995.

Tyler, Kelsey. *It Must Have Been a Miracle*. Berkeley Books, 1995.

VanScott, Miriam. *The Encyclopedia of Heaven*. St. Martin's Press, 1999.

Verne, Jean. *Jules Verne*. Taplinger, 1976.

Wigal, Donald. *Visions of Nostradamus and Other Prophets*. Media Solutions Services, 2002.

White, Ellen G. *The Great Controversy between Christ and Satan*. Pacific Press Publishing.

Wikipedia, "The Free Encyclopedia" The Internet

Wilson, Damon. *The Mammoth Book of Prophecies*. Carral and Graf Publishing, 2003.

Wilson, Ian. *The After Death Experience*. William Morrow and Co. Inc., 1987.

Witherton III, Ben, and Hershel Shanks. *The Brother of Jesus: The Dramatic Story and Meaning of the First Archeological Link to Jesus and His Family*. Harper, San Francisco.

Yogananda, Paramahansa. *Autobiography of a Yogi*. Self-Realization Fellowship, 2005.

Index